Expect Miracles:

CHARTER SCHOOLS AND THE POLITICS OF HOPE AND DESPAIR

Peter W. Cookson, Jr.

and

Kristina Berger

A Member of the Perseus Books Group

Appendix used with courtesy of the Charter Schools Institute–State University of New York (www.newyorkcharters.org).

Westview Press books are available at special discounts or bulk purchases in the United States by corporations, institutions, and other organizations. For more information, please contact the Special Markets Department at the Perseus Books Group, 11 Cambridge Center, Cambridge, MA 02142, or call (617) 252-5298.

Published in 2002 in the United States of America by Westview Press, 5500 Central Avenue, Boulder, Colorado 80301-2877, and in the United Kingdom by Westview Press, 12 Hid's Copse Road, Cumnor Hill, Oxford OX2 9JJ.

Find us on the World Wide Web at www.westviewpress.com.

Library of Congress Cataloging-in-Publication Data
Cookson, Peter W.
   Expect miracles : charter schools and the politics of hope and despair
/ Peter W. Cookson, Jr. and Kristina Berger.
      p. cm.
   Includes bibliographical references and index.
   ISBN 0-8133-6631-3 (hard)
   1. Charter schools--United States. I. Berger, Kristina. II. Title.
LB2806.36.C68 2002
371.01--dc21

                                                                    2002003716

The paper used in this publication meets the requirements of the American National Standard for Permanence of Paper for Printed Library Materials Z39.48-1984.

Printed in the United States of America.
1 2 3 4 5 6 7 8 9 10—05 04 03 02

For
Kai and Teah Wilson, and
Muriel and Robert Berger.

With Love and Gratitude.

Contents

Acknowledgments

We are indebted to the many generous educators who have shared with us their perspectives on charter schools. Their willingness to be frank and generous with their time has informed us and enriched our understanding of charter schools.

We are also grateful to Teachers College for its support, and in particular to Katie Embree and Grace Iida of TC Innovations.

We would also like to thank Steve Catalano and Rebecca Marks of Westview Press for their encouragement and perseverance throughout the project. Judith Serrin was extremely helpful in providing us with excellent editorial suggestions.

Expect Miracles

PROLOGUE:
Faith Versus Reason
in Educational Reform

The idea of the charter school—the inspiration of a handful of educational visionaries—has, in less than fifteen years, become a reform movement of educational and political importance. Classically American, the charter idea emphasizes individualism and promotes a maverick sensibility that suggests that a handful of pioneers can create an imaginative, effective educational system through small-scale local reform. This idea has inspired efforts to redefine accountability, enabled the creation of thousands of new schools, created entirely new private industries (and possibly new fortunes), and catalyzed the passion of thousands of people who had previously been frustrated and dissatisfied with public schools. It is a movement that has many faces and has attracted an eclectic group of proponents and propagandists—justifying a wide range of seemingly contradictory strategies. Laws that support the creation of charter schools have been passed by thirty-seven states and the District of Columbia—and as of September 2001, charter schools were operating in all but three states with charter laws. Despite the charter movement's national reach, however, the geographic distribution of charter schools remains somewhat localized, with just under half of all charter schools currently in operation located in just four states: Arizona, California, Texas, and Michigan. Yet the idea of charter schools—and the promise that they will transform American public education—has captured the nation's imagination.

1

The charter school movement is not only about school reform; it also represents one aspect of a larger social movement that has been significant in American life at least since the election of Ronald Reagan in 1980.[1] In the past two decades there has been a growing consensus, especially among politicians and policymakers, that big government is part of the problem and not part of the solution. Within that context, some have argued strongly that public schools should be deregulated. That is, families should be able to send their child to the public school of their choice—regardless of traditional school zoning regulations. Some deregulators argue that public funds should be used for private schools, and others argue that the public system itself needs to become more flexible, more accountable, and more responsive to families.[2]

The latter position appeals to a wide variety of Americans, as we will discuss throughout this book, for complex and multifaceted reasons. The appeal of charter schools is partly based on the fact that the charter school option plays into some of the major currents that have been shaping American politics for some time. Moreover, charter schools are big-time politics. In 1999 President Bill Clinton addressed the nation about charter schools as follows:

> Charter schools are innovative public schools started by educators, parents and communities, open to students of every background or ability. But they're freer of red tape and top-down management than most of our schools are, and in return for greater flexibility, charter schools must set and meet the highest standards, and stay open only as long as they do. Also, charter schools don't divert taxpayer dollars from our public school system; instead, they use those dollars to promote excellence and competition within the system and in doing so, they spur all our public schools to improve.

Unlike many school reforms, the charter school movement is an intrinsic part of the educational politics of our era and has become a lightning rod in the struggle for the future of public education. This book examines both charter schools and this struggle, because we believe that to understand the rise and possible decline of the charter school movement it is essential to see charter schools in their social, educational, and political contexts.

A charter school is a public school that comes into existence through a contract (charter) with either a state agency or a local school board. The charter establishes the framework within which the school operates and provides public funding for the school for a specified period of time, after which the charter is reviewed and considered for renewal. The charter gives the school's leadership autonomy over its operation and frees the school from many of the regulations that other public schools must follow. In exchange for the flexibility and freedom afforded by the charter, schools are held strictly accountable for helping their students achieve the academic and other performance goals set out in their charter.

An official definition of charter schools, as rendered by the U.S. Department of Education on the www.uscharterschools.org Web site, is as follows:

> Charter schools are nonsectarian public schools of choice that oper-
> ate with freedom from many of the regulations that apply to tradi-
> tional public schools. The "charter" establishing each such school is
> a performance contract detailing the school's mission, program,
> goals, students served, methods of assessment, and ways to measure
> success. The length of time for which charters are granted varies,
> but most are granted for 3–5 years. At the end of the term, the en-
> tity granting the charter may renew the school's contract. Charter
> schools are accountable to their sponsor—usually a state or local
> school board—to produce positive academic results and adhere to
> the charter contract. The basic concept of charter schools is that
> they exercise increased autonomy in return for this accountability.
> They are accountable for both academic results and fiscal practices
> to several groups: the sponsor that grants them, the parents that
> choose them, and the public that funds them. [3]

In theory, charter schools could be a perfect reform strategy, in that they have the potential to transcend the accountability prob-lem (perhaps the most dangerous Achilles heel of the current public school system) and to inspire innovation and reform from within, while empowering teachers and providing parents and children with new and innovative choices. Charter schools, however, have one dangerous loophole. Although they have the potential to renew American public education by providing all children with an equitable and excellent education, charter schools also can be a political wedge that separates public education from the public by creating small schools that cater to a special clientele and thereby further destabilize and deregulate public education.[4]

From our perspective, charter schools, and the movement that supports them, are neither good nor bad. How they are used, by whom, and to what end is what concerns us. Americans tend to see education in evangelical and often moralistic terms. As a nation, we expect schools to provide a level playing field for all children, yet at the same time we have created an educational system that ruthlessly sorts and selects students in theory by merit but in reality most often by class, race, and gender. We expect miracles from our school system, and yet we often avoid the hard policy decisions and the tough political decisions that would make public education truly productive and just.

Another concern we have: those who would use the charter school movement to privatize and monetize a public good. In previous work, Cookson[5] has argued strongly that public education is a public good and that there is a danger in privatizing public education because it removes this public good from democratic accountability. We will touch on this issue throughout this book, but for now suffice it to say that in the long term, we must be careful that both the manifest and latent effects of privatization do not go without discussion or analysis. The spirit of our times is market-oriented. We do not question that markets are efficient at producing goods; we do question whether markets are efficient in the equitable distribution of goods. We also question the long-term political wisdom of privatizing public services in the name of efficiency because, as we will argue later, we believe that social markets are quite different than commodities markets.

Throughout this book, which chronicles the birth and first decade of the charter school movement and an exploration of the political, social, and philosophical ideas that inform and reflect the movement, we will come back to the ideas outlined above. Before we can begin this exploration, however, we want to illustrate the charter school movement in its variety and fullness—its leaders, its schools, its politics, and its business—and characterize its themes, ideas, and philosophies. Subsequently, we will fully discuss charter schools—and the movement's politics of hope and despair.

CHARTER SCHOOLS: CREATED IN THE IMAGE OF THEIR FOUNDERS

The process of creating and opening a charter school is a time-intensive undertaking that requires vision, planning, coalition-building, politicking, perseverance, human and financial resources, and the ability to complete an application and contracting process that can often be daunting.[6]

As an introduction to the charter school phenomena, here are four brief examples of charter schools and one example of an education management organization (EMO) that have all been launched in recent years.

Bronx, New York: Bronx Preparatory Charter School

Founded by a young woman with an Ivy League education, a knack for fundraising, and a libertarian turn-of-mind, Bronx Prep (as it is called in short) opened in September 2000 with one hundred students in grades five and six—and has plans to eventually serve students through grade twelve. The school aims to be a traditional college preparatory school, preparing its students for college and beyond. It draws much of its inspiration from Phillips Exeter

Academy, the well-known New Hampshire boarding school. The school's motto? "Preparation + Focus = Success."

Located, for now, in a former Catholic school in the predominantly African-American and Latino Morrisania section of the South Bronx (though it plans to move into a building of its own design and construction), Bronx Prep offers a curriculum inspired by Mortimer Adler's "Paideia Proposal," which aims to weave the educational philosophies of Horace Mann, John Dewey, and Robert Hutchins into a blueprint for a new American education. The school has received much media attention—*The New York Times* covered the school's first year through an in-depth series and put on its Web site an archive of all the articles in the series, as well as school-related documents, parts of the school's original charter application, and general information about the charter movement nationwide.

Port Huron, Michigan:
Academy for Plastics Manufacturing Technology

The Academy for Plastics Manufacturing Technology is one of more than one hundred charter schools that identify itself as "employer-linked." This term is defined by the U.S. Department of Education's Employer-Linked Charter School Web site as *a special type of public charter school in which an employer organization or network joins with educational entrepreneurs in a collaborative partnership to develop and operate a workworld-informed educational program.*[7] The Port Huron area is home to a number of plastic and mold-making companies—companies that had long found it difficult to identify and attract qualified employees and had previously tried (to no avail) to work with local public schools to create viable training programs. With the passing of Michigan's expansive charter law in 1993, which included financial incentives for the creation of trade academies, a group of businesspeople felt that the time was right for a creating a new approach to a plastics manufacturing vocational program.

And so the Academy for Plastics Manufacturing was born, with the full support of the local school district. The academy opened in fall 1998 with 127 eleventh- and twelfth-grade students and has continued to grow since then. It sees itself as the vanguard of a new model of vocational education, and has the curriculum and focus—and new approach to staffing—to support its claim. Students choose to attend the academy—which operates on a half-day schedule—as they would any district vocational program and continue to take core academic subjects at their "home" school. In addition, many students round out their day with a paid internship at a local plastics manufacturer. One of the most striking results the school reports is that its graduates who go on to jobs in the plastics manufacturing industry average entry-level salaries that are nearly twice the minimum wage—evidence for the school's success, its backers say, that is without question.[8]

Southern California: Choice 2000 Charter School

The Choice 2000 Charter School—a school that conducts its classes entirely online using an interactive platform—serves more than 140 students in grades seven to twelve and is also open to adult students who do not have a high-school diploma. Though Choice 2000 is a virtual school, it is not without structure. Students attend "classes" (with a maximum class size of twenty students) and virtually interact with their teacher and fellow students via the Internet. Teachers present information visually; students ask and answer questions and engage in online discussions. Founded in 1994, Choice 2000 is one of the oldest charter schools in California—and in the entire country. It positions itself as a unique alternative for a wide range of students; according to the school's extensive Web site, Choice 2000 students include those who are ill, those who have not done well in regular classrooms because of learning disabilities or hyperactivity, those who are fearful of the conditions in large public schools, and those who have "gotten in trouble" at regular public schools.

Choice 2000's mission is to "enable students to become self-motivated, competent, lifelong learners equipped with the reading, writing, mathematical, technological and problem solving skills necessary to become contributing members of society in the twenty-first century. Choice 2000 On-Line School will provide the opportunity to achieve a high school diploma through the technologies supporting distance learning."[9] Students are measured in a variety of ways, including teacher assessments and grading, standardized tests, communication with parents, and student portfolios that include their projects and test results. The school is free to any student who lives in one of five Southern California counties—Riverside, San Bernadino, San Diego, Imperial, or Orange—but is closed to students in other California counties. Interestingly, students from out-of-state who wish to enroll may do so, at a cost of $175 per nine-week class, plus any mailing costs associated with getting class materials to and from students. Students must log on to the school's site each day and participate in classes—students who don't are considered truant and subject to disciplinary action, as they would be in any school. In order to promote interaction among students, Choice 2000 sponsors in-person social activities and encourages students to connect with one another.

Arizona: Excel Education Centers, Inc.

"Excel in School. Excel in life." With that slogan, and with a charter issued by the State of Arizona authorizing them to educate up to 1,500 middle and high school students, Excel Education Centers opened seven schools in rural communities across central Arizona between 1995 and 2001. Excel Education Centers offer morning, afternoon, and evening classes on a year-round basis—providing maximum flexibility for students, many of whom hold jobs outside of school and whose average age is fifteen. Excel schools bill themselves as an alternative education experience, and they most certainly are: All coursework is delivered using a computer-based curriculum that enables students to progress at their own pace, supported by specially trained generalist instructors. An individualized instructional program is developed for each student, and the plan can be followed at the student's own pace. Excel students are subject to Arizona state standardized tests, including the Stanford 9 and Arizona's AIMS (Arizona Instrument to Measure the Standards) graduation test.

One integral part of the Excel experience is a mandatory service-learning project that each student must design and complete before graduation. To prepare for the project, students must take two courses—Career Exploration and Job Search Skills—and then they must complete at least fifty hours of service learning in a business or community organization of their choice. Unlike some service-learning programs at middle and high schools across the country, Excel's program is less about community service and more about career preparation, awareness, and planning—though both may be addressed by the student's project. One of the program's explicit goals is to "help the student develop a personal framework for learning decision-making techniques to plan their future educational and career goals."[10] This is in keeping with the school's mission of preparing students for employment by "providing job readiness skills, career decision-making skills, and independent living skills." At Excel schools, students prepare for careers by learning in ways that mirror the workforce—independently, using computers, and interacting with instructor/coaches rather than teachers.

Wall Street, Manhattan, New York City: Mosaica Education

Mosaica Education isn't a school. It's an educational management organization (EMO) founded in 1997 by a businessman who thought that public schools could be run more efficiently by the private sector—and who raised millions of dollars to finance his company in an effort to "get to scale." As of fall 2001, the company operated twenty-one public schools and public charter schools in eight states across the country. In many ways, Mosaica operates like a school district—developing curricula, providing administrative and financial support, procuring and installing technology, hiring administrators, and educating students on a relatively fixed budget. In other ways, however, Mosaica is a business, pure and simple—in 2001, it acquired another EMO, Advantage Schools, which is now a wholly owned subsidiary of Mosaica, with Advantage shareholders receiving Mosaica stock in exchange for their Advantage shares. Mosaica is also a developer of proprietary material—its Paragon Curriculum, which is the curriculum presented each afternoon to students in every Mosaica school—is proprietary material that adds unique value to its schools and is not available to schools outside the Mosaica network.

Some schools Mosaica manages are "regular" public schools, with Mosaica present at the request of a local school district. Others are charter schools, whose leadership has asked Mosaica to come in to run their schools both academically and administratively. Mosaica manages schools with a budget derived from the same level of per-pupil spending as neighboring district schools; one long-term goal is to improve student achievement through technological and pedagogical innovations that enable Mosaica to extract both performance and profits. This is where the concept of "scale" comes in. By making educational infrastructure more cost-effective in ways that public school districts cannot, the argument goes, there will be more money to spend on classroom enhancements that lead to increased student achievement, and also on profits to reward shareholders and institutional investors for taking a risk on the radical concept of privatizing public education.

Mosaica does present its schools as quality educational havens for predominantly urban children—emphasizing the quality of their teachers, the innovation present in their schools and classrooms, and the power of the Paragon Curriculum, which draws its inspiration from the classical canon and integrates interdisciplinary study of art and culture—that will, without a doubt, educate children better than nearby "regular" public schools. But the question is this: What will privatization and profit do to the "regular" public school system over time?

The schools described above represent just a tiny fraction of the estimated 2,357 charter schools in operation as of September 2001.[11] They embody a wide range of educational philosophies and purposes. The Bronx Preparatory Charter School is earnestly trying to provide an excellent prep school education, and all that implies, to under-served South Bronx students, with the hope that this school will position its students to attain previously unheard-of goals. The Academy for Plastics Manufacturing is turning out students— soon to be entry-level workers—who are skilled in techniques of plastic extrusion and mold-making to keep the Port Huron-area plastics industry running. The Choice 2000 Charter School uses technology to connect students who are being educated at home with teachers, students, and a modicum of extracurricular activities and student life. The seven Excel Education Centers present a model of learning that is largely self-directed and that asks students to learn independently from computer-driven courses—and that employs instructors who may not have subject-area mastery, but who can help students with the computer programs. And finally, Mosaica Education, along with its new subsidiary, Advantage Schools, is a corporate school district, essentially running two kinds of schools: Mosaica schools, which place a heavy emphasis on teaching students through the prism of western arts, culture and inquiry, and Advantage schools, which relies heavily on the Direct Instruction method, characterized by heavily scripted lessons with little room for teacher input or improvisation and little leeway for student-driven inquiry and learning.

Across America, charter schools are being founded by groups and individuals intent on escaping the culture—and to some, the tyranny—of traditional public schools. Many of these innovators are talented and able educational pioneers searching for new educational frontiers; others are amateurs or dilettantes, seeking a private

State	Year Charter Law Passed	Estimated number of charter schools as of 9/01
Alaska	1995	15
Arizona	1994	419
Arkansas	1994	6
California	1992	358
Colorado	1993	89
Connecticut	1996	16
Delaware	1995	11
District of Columbia	1996	41
Florida	1996	180
Georgia	1993	46
Hawaii	1994	22
Idaho	1998	11
Illinois	1996	28
Indiana	2001	0
Kansas	1994	28
Louisiana	1995	26
Massachusetts	1993	43
Michigan	1993	196
Minnesota	1991	75
Mississippi	1997	1
Missouri	1998	22
Nevada	1997	9
New Hampshire	1995	0
New Jersey	1996	55
New Mexico	1993	21
New York	1998	32
North Carolina	1996	96
Ohio	1997	68
Oklahoma	1999	10
Oregon	1999	17
Pennsylvania	1997	77
Rhode Island	1995	6
South Carolina	1996	8
Texas	1995	214
Utah	1998	9
Virginia	1998	6
Wisconsin	1993	96
Wyoming	1995	0
Total		2357

Years that charter laws passed, by state, with estimated number of charter schools currently in operation.

Source: Center for Education Reform

educational fiefdom in which their philosophy and vision—good, bad, or indifferent—will go largely unchallenged.

The evolution of charter schools is also an object lesson in the contradictory forces that underlie American public education: public versus corporate accountability; entrepreneurial versus bureaucratic spirit; consumer versus community motives; self versus public interest. These forces, in seeming opposition to one another, have succeeded in driving the bar of excellence in education higher, even in the face of what appears to be declining educational performance among many children and the questionable efficacy of our schools. In fact, by expanding the reach of schools over the last century and raising our educational goals, we have, arguably, made excellence for all harder to attain for all children.

THE CHARTER SCHOOL PROMISE

Exactly how are charter schools going to revolutionize public education? How will they, in the words of Joe Nathan, stimulate the larger system to improve?[12] Proponents of the charter concept believe that charter schools, by virtue of their independence from the system and the innovation that supporters believe will be the hallmark of each school, will revolutionize the entire public school system one school at a time. They believe that charter schools will solve issues of equity and accountability that have for years gone unsolved. They believe that charter schools will inspire new levels of family and community involvement. They believe that charter schools will reinvigorate teachers, improve the quality of teaching, and boost student achievement through a combination of innovative teaching strategies and increased attention to individual students. In fact, the fathers of the charter school movement (virtually all of the original charter school champions are men) pretty much believe that charter schools represent the holy grail of the education reform movement—the cup from which all who hope to improve public education, locally or systemically, must drink. With fervor and conviction, Joe Nathan and others began to spread the gospel of charter schools with the evangelical zeal of revivalist preachers.[13]

What specifically are these claims, and how do the movement's proponents believe charter schools will fulfill them? On the following pages, we examine the major claims made in support of the charter school movement's ability to fix the problems of the American public school system. We will also begin to raise questions about these claims—but will not return to evaluate the outcomes of the movement until later in this book, when we will compare promises made to the realities of today's charter school movement.

The original apostles of the charter school movement argued that charter schools would promote innovation and support the sharing of best practices among charter schools and between charter schools and traditional public schools, thereby spurring change throughout the entire system. One of the recurring themes in the rhetoric of the charter school movement is that under most existing bureaucracies, true innovation and independence is impossible and that this tyranny can be blamed for at least part of the current crisis in education. Who's responsible for this repressive environment? Opponents of the current system blame the system itself—remember, government is the enemy of innovation. Burdensome paperwork prevents teachers from creating new lesson plans. The archaic structure of the daily schedule at most public schools prevents collaboration and cross-fertilization among teachers—and between teachers at different schools. Meddling school leadership—in this scenario, teachers and administrators are enemies, not allies—creates an environment in which teachers are discouraged from trying anything new. Union rules prevent teachers from spending extra time at school or participating on after-hours school leadership teams. District-wide initiatives that require schools to use a single set of textbooks and approved curricula remove local control over what is taught from teachers and parents.

Under charter schools, however, proponents promised that all the barriers described above would be shattered, resulting in miraculous educational gains: Schools would no longer be indentured to local school districts. The amount of time-consuming paperwork would be reduced—and teachers would be free of all associated burdens, giving them the time and freedom to innovate and inspire. Locally designed schools would allow for the creation of innovative scheduling plans; schools would be free to choose their own curricula and subject areas. Locally developed educational philosophies and strategies would enable schools to more personally address the needs of their students, making them uniquely able to help students achieve. Charter schools would be the magic bullet that teachers had been waiting years for—and with empowered teachers, students would automatically, almost miraculously, do better. Charter schools, because of their ability to specialize, would be able to serve special populations of students far better than regular public schools could—and would therefore be more attractive to parents and students.

Other claims by the movement's proponents about the change that charter schools would bring include:

Charter schools would create a truly equitable system of public education.

Building on the idea that more specialized, "custom designed" schools would be better able to educate even the most challenging—and challenged—students, charter school supporters claimed that charter schools would address—and solve—equity issues in public education more effectively than any previously tried educational reform strategy. It is a long-held belief—though to some, it is a long-held myth—that American public schools have the potential to be the great equalizer, able to provide all students with the keys to their own personal American Dream. It is also a long-noticed reality that American public schools are not currently living up to this myth and that many children and young adults who attend our public schools graduate (or worse, drop out) without the tools and knowledge necessary to live their dream.

In a successful public school system, all students would be provided with an equal potential to succeed regardless of their race, ethnicity, gender, socio-economic status, parental education levels, or geographical location. Schools that are successful at addressing equity issues among their students are able to produce students who perform well regardless of their status. The charter school gospel holds that because schools will be smaller, more free to customize educational experiences to the needs of the students they serve, and better able to engage parents and communities in the business of educating their young, they will be more likely to overcome barriers to equal educational opportunity.

Interestingly, the pro-equity argument is offered by charter school supporters without regard to how schools intend to recruit and define their student populations. Technically, charter schools are required to enroll students without restriction—that is, they cannot explicitly select the best students, require passing scores on entrance examinations, or place restrictions on admissions. Charter schools are supposed to enroll students just as a neighborhood public school would—on a first-come, first-served basis, with randomized admission by lottery in situations where demand for a school exceeds the number of students it can accommodate.

In reality, this is not always the case. Some charter schools specifically reach out to at-risk students—indeed, many states give preference to charter applications from schools that propose to serve this population—concentrating the most difficult students in a single school. Other schools offer a narrowly defined curriculum, attracting only a narrow segment of potential students. This phenomenon raises a question: Can a school that, for whatever reason, has a narrowly defined student body truly expect to make equity strides? Are schools that narrowly define success—and that may only provide skills or experiences that funnel students into a single profession—really doing anything to provide equitable access to all levels of society to all students they educate?

Charter schools would improve student performance.

Most charter schools are substantially smaller than traditional public schools—according to a recent study, the average number of students per charter school during the 2000–2001 school year was approximately 250.[14] There is convincing research that smaller schools are a more effective educational environment for students than are larger schools. It is this smaller, more personalized environment that most charter school proponents touted as the reason that charter schools would be able to elicit improved academic performance from the students they serve. By supporting the creation of schools that are structurally able to follow the popular educational theory that "smaller is better"—as espoused by Ted Sizer and others—the charter school movement was jumping on the bandwagon of an already popular educational movement.

Charter schools would strengthen the market movement in education—thereby strengthening the entire system.

For the reasons stated earlier, proponents claimed that charter schools would obviously be better than non-charter public schools. In theory, the more "good" schools there are, the more students they will attract—and the fewer students left attending not-so-good schools. Shrinking student populations will inspire these poorer schools to improve—and if they are not successful, school districts will force them to close. Charter schools would, therefore, inspire the entire system to improve—the epitome of the benevolent market in action.

Charter schools would provide better models for school accountability.

Charter schools are contractually bound to state-sponsored chartering agencies to turn out students who are able to pass state-administered standardized tests. If the schools don't, they risk losing their charter. Under the charter system, it is theorized that schools will seek to maximize the number of students who pass these tests—thereby ensuring the schools' survival. However, does this mean that charter schools are even more likely to teach to the test—in spite of simultaneous claims that charter schools are home to innovative curricula and creative educational strategies? Or that achievement, in a charter school, is defined most importantly by how well a student performs on a standardized test?

Perhaps. But is this healthy? Of course, the charter school accountability-for-autonomy bargain assumes that state chartering agencies have clear definitions of the achievement standard for charter schools—and that they not only articulate this standard, but choose to enforce it when schools' charters come up for renewal.

Another aspect of accountability for charter schools is fiscal accountability. Under a charter system, each school's administration is responsible for all aspects of financial management of the school. There is no longer a district to fall back onto for payroll systems, budget support, coordination of applications for federal education funds, and technology infrastructure.

Charter schools must also comply with all federal civil rights laws and all applicable regulations under the Americans with Disabilities Act. Compliance in these areas is often difficult for traditional public schools; is it any easier—or more difficult—for charters?

Charter schools would forge improved links with families and communities.

Charter schools claim to be uniquely able to reflect the values and priorities of the community that creates and sustains them. This is one of the most attractive aspects of the charter movement—the possibility of creating and/or sending your children to a school that reflects your cultural and educational values. But does this also mean that charter schools are likely to serve narrowly defined interest groups or student populations—defeating the concept of the common school that has historically been so integral to the success of our democratic society?

With the potential to make revolutionary improvements in all of the above areas—and more—charter schools were presented as a revolutionary—yet viable—large-scale educational reform strategy.

The leap from theory to practice was a quick one. Within two years of the nation's first charter school, which opened in St. Paul, Minnesota, in 1992, ten additional states had passed legislation enabling the establishment of charter schools.

Brett Lane, a researcher for the Northwest Regional Educational Laboratory (NWREL), presented the charter school movement as a movement "plagued by inconsistency and uncertainty," and a "diverse and confusing collection of values, motives, beliefs, and assumptions."[15] To Lane, charter schools present a challenge to policymakers in that there are many goals that could be reached by expanding charter schools—but bad or poorly defined charter schools could have long-term negative effects on the system as a whole. In his analysis of the movement, Lane characterized four perspectives within the charter school movement on the purposes of this reform strategy: (1) charter schools as the catalyst for systemic change; (2) charter schools as a component of comprehensive education reform; (3) charter schools as a means to enhance educational equity; and (4) charter schools as a means to enhance group equity.

The charter school movement is part of the larger school choice movement. The school choice movement is the struggle between those who believe families should be able to choose the schools their children attend and those who believe in the "common" school, where all the children in a neighborhood are assigned a school by the local educational authority. We will discuss the issue of school choice throughout this book, but suffice it to say here that school choice arouses public passion because beyond public policy issues, the issue of school choice is a litmus test for what people believe most deeply about education, about society, and about the prospects for freedom.

THE POLITICS OF HOPE AND DESPAIR

As we develop our analysis, the title of this book will become clearer. For now, let us just say that, in general, many Americans have succumbed to wishful thinking when it comes to school improvement—hence, we have come to expect miracles rather than to plan for change and to challenge the entrenched interests that keep our highly stratified school system in place.[16]

The second part of the title refers to the intense and often obscure politics that form the larger framework of educational reform. We are living in a period when politics, especially national politics, has become increasingly pervasive in education. Unsure about our national purpose or the soundness of our public institutions, we vacillate between hope and despair. We hope that our public institutions, particularly our public schools, will provide the safety and the mobility we need to keep creating a viable democracy. We despair of our public institutions because they are perceived to be inefficient, slow moving, and sometimes corrupt. Perhaps part of the despair is that we expect miracles from public institutions and are extremely quick to find fault with them, even as we are quite forgiving of the private sector. Thus the United States Congress feels comfortable in bailing out the Savings and Loan industry through legislation that is passed with hardly any dissent—but cannot find the wherewithal to bail out the failing public schools, especially the public schools that serve the poorest children.

This critique of the larger political and social environment informs our discussion of charter schools. Without making a clearer connection between school and society, all analysis is bound to be superficial, because schools proceed from society and reflect society. Too often, educational reformers speak and write as though society is healthy and schools are sick; but logic does not require such a proposition. The problems of schools are the problems of society. The charter school movement is as much about symbolic politics as it is about "school reform." It is our hope that our analysis not only adds to the literature concerning charter schools, but that it also contributes to a larger understanding of the relationship between school and society.

We believe that the United States has the capacity to create a universal, free and just public school system. While this book is about charter schools, we do touch on some of the design principles that we believe would make for such a school system. We examine charter schools against this criteria, but we also recognize that no individual or groups of individuals can be accountable for all the problems of public education. We applaud those who wish to create a more productive and just school system by founding government-sponsored alternative schools but cannot shake the suspicion that small acts of reform do little to genuinely alter the system.

In Part One, we describe the charter school movement in some detail and in Part Two, we analyze the reasons behind the charter school movement. We finish with a postscript that tackles the difficult problem of what it would take to create a democratic education for all students.

PART ONE:
The Landscape of Charter Schools

THE EDUCATIONAL AND SOCIAL CONTEXT OF THE
CHARTER SCHOOL MOVEMENT

The charter school movement's ability to capture the imagination and support of a broad and influential spectrum of American society—from grassroots community groups to Fortune 500 executives, from politicians to parents—is a testament not only to the power of the charter school idea itself but also to the gravity of the problems, both real and imagined, that the movement's champions promised that charter schools would solve. When the movement first took shape, in the late 1980s and early 1990s, the ground was extremely fertile for new ideas in education reform. The public school system was under sharp criticism for failing to educate America's children to "world class" standards; despite nearly a decade of frenzied activity to address the concerns raised in 1983's *A Nation At Risk* report,[1] little progress—as measured by performance on standardized tests—had been made.

Over the past twenty years, frustration with what to many appears to be a stagnating system has fueled the push for charter schools as well as for many other, even more radical, reform concepts, including vouchers and privately funded scholarship programs for low-income children. Looking even further back, however, we can see the charter school movement's roots in the educational and social reform movements of the 1960s and 1970s. The potential for change and reform inherent in the idea of charter schools—local control of schools, elimination of bureaucracy, independence, and entrepreneurism—is one of the reasons it has such broad support.

This appeal is part of a broad social and educational movement called school choice. School choice plans and policies took root long before the charter idea came along. When the charter idea emerged, the choice movement, recognizing an attractive option, quickly embraced charters as perhaps the most broadly acceptable choice plan possible—and perhaps its ticket to wholesale acceptance.

Although the variety of school choice plans makes summarization difficult, a few major types can be identified. Some choice plans partially restrict the educational choices families can make, while others have virtually no restrictions. The former type of plan is often referred to as "controlled choice" and the latter as "open enrollment." Most choice plans fall near the middle of the continuum between the two types. Below are some basic choice definitions:

Intradistrict choice: A plan that allows students to choose schools within a single public school district. Depending on the specific plan, the range of choice may be limited to a few schools within a district or it may encompass every school within the district.

Interdistrict choice: A plan in which students may cross district lines to attend school. Tuition funds from the state follow the student, and transportation costs—to get students to the school of their choice—are usually covered by state funds. Unlimited interdistrict choice is functionally equivalent to statewide open enrollment.

Intrasectional choice: A plan that is limited to public schools.

Intersectional choice: A plan that includes both public and private or parochial schools.

Controlled choice: A student assignment plan that requires families to choose a school within a given community, but that also reserves the right to restrict choices to ensure the racial, gender, and socio-economic balance of each school. Often, such plans reflect a strategy to satisfy court-ordered desegregation requirements.

Magnet schools: Public schools that offer specialized programs, often deliberately designed and located so as to attract students to otherwise unpopular areas or schools. Magnet schools are often created specifically to promote racial balance within a given school.

Postsecondary options: Programs that enable high school students to enroll in college courses at government expense. The courses they take may be used to satisfy high school graduation requirements as well as count toward college credits.

Second-chance programs: Alternative schools and programs for students who have had difficulties in standard public school settings. Most often these students have either dropped out of school, are pregnant or are parents, have been assessed as chemically dependent, or have been expelled from their previous school(s).

Charter schools. Publicly sponsored but autonomous schools that are substantially free of direct administrative control by the government but are held accountable for achieving certain levels of student performance and meeting other specified outcome goals.

Workplace training: Apprenticeship programs to teach students a skilled trade not offered through present vocational training. Costs are divided between the employer and the school district.

Voucher plans: Any system of certificate or cash payments by the government that enables public school students to attend the public or non-public school of their choice. Vouchers have a fixed value and are redeemed at the time of enrollment.

Tuition tax credits: A system of funding school choice that allows parents to receive credit against their income tax if they choose to send their child to a non-public school. Such a system is, by definition, one that supports intersectional choice.

Source: Peter W. Cookson, Jr., *School Choice: The Struggle for the Soul of American Education*. Yale University Press 1994

As we can see from the above definitions, tailoring a choice plan is itself a creative endeavor. Choice can be limited to one district and thus have minimal educational design consequences, or it can be statewide and intersectional and thus completely alter the way schools are organized within a state. Nobody has yet proposed an interstate choice plan and, as far as we know, nobody has seriously suggested a classroom choice plan.

The Early Years

The school choice movement has its roots in educational reform theory and practice that dates to the early 1970s, when sociologist Christopher Jencks wrote a report for the federal Office of Economic Opportunity that proposed a voucher program that would enable parents of public school children to choose the school—public or private—that their child would attend.[2] Each parent would receive a voucher, representing a child's portion of education funding, to be presented at the selected school; the plan provided for additional dollars to be added to the vouchers of poorer children, to encourage schools to accept these students as well as to recognize the necessity (and the cost) of additional educational resources for them.[3] Not surprisingly, the proposal met with fierce resistance from civil liberties groups—who argued that by allowing students to use public dollars to support their private or parochial education the government was blurring the line between church and state. National and local teachers unions also opposed the idea, partially driven by the fear that a voucher would weaken the role of teachers and teachers unions in public schools and even jeopardize the jobs of some members (if a school was unpopular and failed to attract students—and funding—it would necessarily close, leaving its staff out of work). And, like civil rights groups, many teachers and teachers unions believed that vouchers would weaken the public education system as a whole.

A single public school district responded to the government's call for participation in this pilot program. California's Alum

Rock district, a racially diverse district located to the east of San Jose, became the first to experiment with this voucher system, though a first step for the district was to implement school-based reforms to re-shape academic programs and to create a more diverse set of academic choices. The Alum Rock voucher initiative was eventually implemented, but ended up being more about school decentralization, a priority of the district's then-superintendent. The school district directed financial and other incentives to schools that allowed for the creation of innovative mini-school programs that would serve narrowly defined groups of students.

To die-hard voucher supporters, the Alum Rock experiment was a failure, as it failed to transcend the status quo, as they saw it, of the existing public school bureaucracy.[4] To those looking for the roots of the charter movement, however, it is an interesting milestone because it represents one of the first times that the concept of school-determined program design and development, coupled with a system of choice, was touted as a core component of an effective systemic reform movement. And, though vouchers as we know them today were not tested in Alum Rock, this early voucher plan was among the first, if not the first, to incorporate public school choice as a mechanism to address issues of economic and ethnic inequality.

During the 1970s, magnet schools (schools that embrace and promote a specific theme, reflect a specific teaching philosophy, or are targeted to meet the needs of a specific subgroup of students, such as the gifted or the visually impaired, and that are, by definition, schools of choice)[5] began to arrive on the scene. They represented a creative, innovative, and school-centered spirit in public education as well as the instrument for a number of notable school desegregation plans, both court-ordered and self-imposed. Whatever the reason for their emergence in a given district, magnet schools aimed to provide more diverse educational choices for students and became havens for teachers and educators who wanted an environment in which to present and express new educational models and program designs.

We mention magnet schools in our survey of charter school precursors because they are an example of a school improvement strategy that is both systemic—in that school systems often turned to the magnet strategy to improve, desegregate, or diversify their educational programs—and school-based, in that many magnet schools and academic programs were developed internally by the school's team of educators and often (though not always) embodied a creative, almost maverick spirit that energized parents, faculty, and communities. In other words, many magnet schools developed similarly to the way charter schools later would—in an environment where educators and teachers, and sometimes parents, were given the opportunity and resources to create educational institutions that reflected local and personal goals and philosophies. However, core charter concepts, such as the autonomy-accountability trade-off and the nearly complete separation from local districts and boards of education, had not yet emerged at the time that magnet schools were gaining popularity.

The voucher idea stayed on the table throughout the 1980s, gaining support—and enemies. Early voucher efforts were supported mainly by the conservative right and the Catholic school lobby (driven by self-interest and self-preservation as much as anything), and to a lesser extent by civil rights groups who believed that voucher programs would result in a more equitable educational landscape, as poor families would have the financial resources to make the same types of educational choices (for example, to opt out of the public school system) that middle and upper class families have for their children.

The pro-voucher argument is based on the assumption that competitive market forces, coupled with the power of the dollar, would move the public school system to a place where good schools would be financially rewarded, bad schools would go bankrupt and close, and if dollars moved out of the public system to private schools, so be it—if the professional educators don't want the system fixed, then let the people speak. And if the people speak in such a way that the government ceases to be the dominant force in public education, so be it as well.

From the beginning, however, little serious attention was paid to the potential negative consequences of voucher systems: What would happen to children whose families did not or could not make good choices about where to send their children? What would be the social and cultural consequences of a policy that indirectly advocates for the removal of public education from public hands? If schools fail because they fail to attract customers, what happens to the children who are left behind? Rational market theory claims that the consumer mentality will ensure that every child ends up in a school that is good for her and that in the long haul, only "good" schools will survive—but as we know all too well from personal experience, and as empirical economists are beginning to document, personal behavior is not always rational.[6]

While the voucher movement developed, so did the school choice movement—often, but not always, hand-in-hand. Though some embraced expanded school choice plans as an acceptable compromise for (and hopeful precursor to) more extensive voucher initiatives, it turned out that interest in school choice was not limited to those people or communities who were interested in establishing a system of voucher-funded education. In fact, many school districts and educational reform groups saw choice as a way to increase parental confidence and involvement in the system; many parents saw public school choice as a policy that would enable them to play a more active role in their children's education.

Indeed, for years, informal school choice had existed across the country—with parents with means able to choose the neighborhood they live in (and therefore the school district), able to locate exceptional public school programs (and pull the strings of privilege to enroll their children), able to afford private or parochial schools, and able to devote the time to find and enroll their children in the program or school of their choice. All of these choice-related efforts are more likely to be undertaken by parents with means; the expansion of public school choice promised the potential to extend these opportunities to parents of all income levels. By extension, public school choice, if undertaken from the standpoint of its value as an internal reform strategy, and in such a way that it strengthens and expands quality and equitable education for all children, is a reform strategy for public education that offers the possibilities of increased educational justice.

The 1980s

Market and choice-based strategies to reform public education, which took root in the 1980s, emerged in response to a new faith in business models and a growing distrust of the government's ability to do anything right. Coupled with a new faith in markets was a new sense of urgency about the need for educational reform.[7]

The 1983 report *A Nation At Risk*, prepared by the National Commission on Excellence in Education, at the request of T. H. Bell, then the Secretary of Education, raised serious concerns about the ability of American public schools to graduate students who would be able to compete with their counterparts from other countries and contribute to American excellence and international supremacy. The report's introduction painted a devastating portrait of our educational system:

> Our Nation is at risk. Our once unchallenged preeminence in commerce, industry, science, and technological innovation is being overtaken by competitors throughout the world. This report is concerned with only one of the many causes and dimensions of the problem, but it is the one that undergirds American prosperity, security, and civility. We report to the American people that while we can take justifiable pride in what our schools and colleges have historically accomplished and contributed to the United States and the well-being of its people, the educational foundations of our society are presently being eroded by a rising tide of mediocrity that threatens our very future as a Nation and a people. What was unimaginable a generation ago has begun to occur—others are matching and surpassing our educational attainments.
>
> If an unfriendly foreign power had attempted to impose on America the mediocre educational performance that exists today, we

might well have viewed it as an act of war. As it stands, we have allowed this to happen to ourselves. We have even squandered the gains in student achievement made in the wake of the Sputnik challenge. Moreover, we have dismantled essential support systems, which helped make those gains possible. We have, in effect, been committing an act of unthinking, unilateral educational disarmament.[8]

This ambitious report, which turned out to be profoundly influential, if not ultimately effective, contained data that showed that the achievement levels of American students had declined precipitously in comparison with their counterparts around the world, and presented this fact as something that needed to be aggressively counteracted in order for the United States to regain international stature. The report's summary of research on the state of American public education focused on four areas—content, expectations, time, and teaching—and featured negative and alarming statistics. The report's authors outlined specific recommendations about policy and suggested changes that could be made to help our public education system improve.

Though some considered the report alarmist, it nonetheless inspired politicians, business leaders, and prominent educators to make public pronouncements of support and to step up efforts to reform public education. *A Nation At Risk* provided powerful ammunition to those who argued that the progressive educational reform experiments of the 1970s had weakened, not strengthened, the American educational infrastructure. It also lent credence to those who would take a back-to-basics approach, further cementing the liberal versus conservative struggle over the soul of American public education that, like many similar Reagan-era conflicts, would nearly be won—outright or, later, through compromise—by conservative forces.

Interestingly, though not surprisingly, *A Nation At Risk* fails to explore the intractable connection between the problems of school and the problems of society—and does not explore or connect non-school issues like poverty, family employment, or education

with student performance. Because *A Nation at Risk* does not acknowledge these forces, it fails to recommend educational or social
policy solutions to these challenges or to address the root causes of
the achievement gap between rich and poor that had so greatly
widened in the 1970s and that continues to grow. Instead, the recommendations that follow from the report's narrow focus on student achievement outcomes necessarily suggests improvement
strategies that involve improved or enhanced curricula, increasingly stringent and frequently administered achievement tests,
and a back-to-basics pedagogical approach. Ironically, nearly two
decades after *A Nation at Risk*'s publication, federal education reform strategies, like those espoused by President George W. Bush,
are eerily similar, but for the fact that the system is twenty years
older and the sociological causes of the achievement gap have
grown even more complex and difficult to address.

Perhaps the first person to publicly describe the idea of a charter
school was Albert Shanker. Shanker, who started his career as a
substitute mathematics teacher in a public elementary school in
East Harlem, New York City, was elected president of New York
City's United Federation of Teachers (UFT) union in 1964 and of the
American Federation of Teachers (AFT) in 1974. He served in both
roles concurrently and was a powerful national and international
labor leader and educational visionary for nearly four decades.

Shanker rose to national prominence in the mid-1960s, when
turmoil in New York City's schools turned classrooms and communities into battlegrounds for teachers and civil rights activists. At
issue was a conflict between the leaders of an experiment in community control of schools—one aspect of which was the desire to
have additional control over what teachers would teach in the
schools under the local school board's control—and the teachers in
those schools who did not believe that a local school board had the
right to remove them from teaching positions to which they had
been assigned. Shanker's UFT supported the teachers; soon, the

conflict that had arisen in the predominantly African-American and low-income Brooklyn community of Ocean Hill-Brownsville spread to the entire city, setting off a citywide teachers strike that ended only when Mayor John Lindsay stepped in and settled the strike with decisions that were overwhelmingly favorable to the UFT (even while establishing a system of locally controlled school boards that would oversee elementary and middle schools).

In the years following the strike, Shanker became a nationally prominent educator. For many years Shanker wrote and placed, on behalf of the AFT, an editorial advertisement in each edition of the Sunday *New York Times* that served as a weekly synopsis of the UFT's position on the most pressing educational issues of the day. Shanker's, and the AFT's, politics were consistently pro-union and pro-public education. Though Shanker had a great and innovative mind, he was also a great and innovative union leader; he tried never to let his policies undermine the strength of his union and the union movement.

At a 1988 Minnesota conference on school reform, and later that year in a speech at the National Press Club, Shanker sung the praises of a new idea in school reform, the charter school. This idea was formulated by a former schoolteacher, Ray Budde, and had been described in a report entitled *Education by Charter: Restructuring School Districts*.[9] As presented by Shanker, charter schools were a new kind of school governance framework under which successful teachers would become "empowered" to create innovative programs at existing schools—but only with the express approval of their union. Taken one step further, charter schools, as originally conceived, would become places where teachers would be recognized as experts and, given the freedom to follow their own educational visions, would surely make schools better places for teachers to teach and more effective environments for students to learn. To Shanker, the charter school was a teacher-centered reform strategy that would inspire reform from the inside. Teachers would be unrestricted by regulations and free to innovate and build new educational models based on student needs and on shared best practices.[10]

By giving teachers—the experts in the trenches—more authority over the schools they taught in and more freedom from restrictive rules and regulations, schools would be transformed. This proposal assumes that teachers, merely by virtue of their desire to innovate, are qualified to create new educational models and programs. From Shanker's perspective, it was the system, not the teachers, that was responsible for the failure of American public schools; by breaking the grip of the system, more satisfied teachers would, in turn, mean better schools—which in turn would result in better-educated students.

However, Shanker's concept of the charter school was not to be the final word. Rather, it was just the beginning. From today's perspective, it is ironic that Shanker, defender of teachers' rights and to a large extent of traditional public school governance structures, was the first person to publicly present and promote the charter concept. As the movement took root, and the charter concept evolved, Shanker would distance himself from the movement that was inspired by the charter school concept—especially as the movement developed an aversion to teachers unions and a tendency to support legislation that would substantially weaken the traditional union-protected rights of teachers, such as tenure and seniority. Interestingly, Albert Shanker had also, years earlier, expressed initial support for and interest in the Alum Rock voucher experiment, but backed away as the voucher idea grew to include policies that would potentially lead to the flow of public dollars into private hands.

Shanker's charter school idea appealed to many educators and reformers and began to develop as a school-based reform strategy. It did not seek to divorce schools from districts or to change the relationship between teachers, unions, and schools. Nor, in fact, did it encompass most of the tenets of today's charter school movement. But because it did seek to question the structures upon which the traditional, failing system was based, the concept opened the door to even more radical questions. Not least of all, Shanker's idea had a catchy name—a marketer's dream. The word "charter" connotes exclusivity and innovation, the concept of firstness, independence, and professionalism—all of which the movement's founders sought to convey.

Shanker did not continue to champion the charter idea for long, as his dual—and in this case, contradictory—roles as an innovative educational thinker and as the president of one of the nation's most powerful teachers unions came into conflict. In the end, Shanker's loyalty remained with the union he led, not the movement he helped create. By 1994, Shanker wrote that, "at best, (charter schools are) a partial answer to the problems that afflict our schools."[11] He was skeptical of claims that charters would eventually revolutionize and improve all of public education, that the market forces that would result from the introduction of charter schools could cure all of the system's many ails. With the inevitable dichotomy of curriculum, culture, and pedagogy among charter schools, Shanker felt that "the basic premise of charter schools ensures that whatever common ground schools now share will disappear" and that "charter schools allow a lot of scope for enthusiasm, but they will leave untouched many of the biggest problems facing our schools."[12]

Shanker ceased to support the burgeoning charter movement when it changed from a teacher-centered, school-based educational improvement strategy that would be implemented within the existing system to a movement that many of its supporters believed was the critical first step toward dismantling the troubled public education establishment. How did this transformation take place? How was a new paradigm of public education created that claimed the ability to equitably and effectively—and successfully—educate all children to academic proficiency and beyond? For answers, we must look to the state of Minnesota, the birthplace of school choice.

The Minnesota Mystique

Just as the story of charter schools cannot be told without exploring its roots in the school choice movement, it also cannot be told without first introducing its homeland, Minnesota; its political godfather, Rudy Perpich; its hero, Joe Nathan; and its elder statesman, Ted Kolderie.

Minnesota has long been a progressive outpost in the otherwise conservative Midwest, and it was here that the seeds of the school choice, charter school, and voucher movements took root.[13] As far back as 1958, when the state enacted legislation that allowed parents who chose to send their children to private schools to take a tuition tax deduction off their state income taxes, Minnesota had begun to test the waters of expanded school choice.[14] Like most states, however, Minnesota required most students who wished to enroll in public schools to attend the school to which they were assigned.

All politics are local—and in the 1970s, this lesson was driven home by the impact that the state policy had on a newly elected government official. Rudy Perpich, the new lieutenant governor, found himself outraged that he could not, by law, transfer his daughter from the public school to which she had been assigned (and that he was dissatisfied with) to a different public school of his choosing. Able to translate his anger and frustration not only into action but into political power, Perpich rallied a group of state legislators who were also interested in school choice. For good measure, he got business involved, with the Minnesota Business Partnership signing on as a supporter of Perpich's efforts to establish school choice options in Minnesota.[15] In 1976, Perpich was elected governor. Soon thereafter, school choice was a front-burner issue in Minnesota, with a wide range of school choice options available to parents, presented as part of a larger, statewide "access to excellence" educational improvement program.

At first, these new school choice options only enabled Minnesota parents to select schools within their local school district. Though their children were no longer tied to a specific neighborhood school, their choices were limited to schools within their assigned district. However, more radical education reform forces in Minnesota started to press for a more controversial form of school choice: statewide open-enrollment, which would allow families to choose to send their children to any school in the state. Ultimately, these advocates became the core of the "radical decentralization" movement that believed that the only solution to the education dilemma was to cut schools free from governmental control and put the power to control public education into the hands of the people.

Joe Nathan, another Minnesotan, was one of the original advocates for the charter school idea and, as of 2002, is a loud, passionate, and utterly dedicated supporter of charter schools and related educational reform efforts. Nathan began his career as a teacher, was actively involved in the alternative schools and civil rights movement of the 1960s, and in 1990 became the founding director of the Center for School Change at the Hubert H. Humphrey Institute of Public Affairs at the University of Minnesota. Nathan built his career on his deep-seated belief that American public education needs out-of-the box reform ideas to have any hope of effectively educating our nation's children, and he is highly critical of the current educational system. He is a ubiquitous and energetic presence in the charter movement, coaching and mentoring charter school founders, political supporters, and researchers across the country.

Despite his unfettered disdain for the bureaucracy and governmental control that in his mind have ruined American public schools, Nathan remains opposed to opening choice plans to include private or parochial schools and does not support vouchers. And in his own way, Nathan is a tireless supporter of and cheerleader for free, public education—albeit within a system that eschews bureaucracy, rewards independence, and judges schools on the basis of outcomes and accountability alone. On a 1999 NPR radio broadcast, Nathan described his views on the charter movement: "The fundamental purpose [of the charter movement] is to expand opportunity, especially for low and moderate income families who currently don't have much. And secondly, to help stimulate improvement in the larger education system." Later in the broadcast, Nathan described a recent National Charter School Conference, where both Democratic and Republican elected and federal officials offered their unqualified support of charter efforts, "I think one of the things that we've seen around the country is that people can disagree about a lot of things, but they agree that the charter movement really makes sense in many, many places if it's done carefully."[16]

Ted Kolderie, a policy analyst and author from Minnesota, was, like Joe Nathan, an early advocate for charter schools and an intense critic of the existing system of bureaucratic and governmental control over public schools. Kolderie's support for charter schools reflected his belief that government should not be the exclusive franchise for managing and controlling public schools. By enabling outside groups, through charter laws, to establish public schools free from direct public control, public schools would embrace innovation as a means to differentiate themselves to attract students. By advocating for charter legislation in Minnesota and elsewhere, Kolderie was challenging the assumption that direct government control of schools is the one best model for our country's public education system.

In his 1990 report, *Beyond Choice to New Public Schools: Withdrawing the Exclusive Franchise in Public Education*, Kolderie proposed a bold new idea: that the way public education is structured—with the process of school districting creating boundaries within which schools are placed and students are assigned—leads to a system in which education is "organized as a pattern of these territorial exclusive franchises."[17] From Kolderie's perspective, there is an inherent problem with the way that school districts are funded and held accountable. Though state and local dollars flow to school districts—funds without which these districts would not be able to operate—states and local governments have an extremely limited ability to cut off the flow of money to districts that don't utilize the money to perform well and produce well-educated students.

Under the current system, states can't easily decide—at least, not without a protracted court battle—to stop funding a failing district and instead direct dollars to another district structure that would be more effective. In short, "An organization with an exclusive franchise is under little pressure to change." Kolderie's proposed solution: to withdraw the exclusive franchise from the school district by enabling other organizations to sponsor public schools, thereby providing parents and students with choices, and perhaps acting as an external agent that would motivate traditional districts and schools to improve. And with a system of strict accountability, defined by student performance, schools would, theoretically, be faced with a straightforward goal against which their existence would be measured.

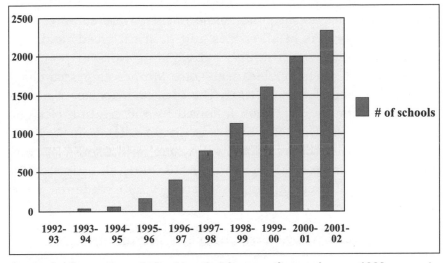

Approximate number of charter schools operating each year, 1992-present
Source: Center for Education Reform

In just eleven years, Kolderie's then-radical proposal was adopted, to varying degrees, by thirty-eight legislatures—thirty-seven states plus the District of Columbia—and the charter movement moved into the mainstream. Though others—Joe Nathan and Jeanne Allen (president of the Washington, D.C.-based, pro-charter Center for Education Reform), for example, have taken a more prominent role in the promotion of charter schools, Kolderie remained a presence in the movement. At the 2000 National Charter Schools Conference, sponsored by the U.S. Department of Education and held in Washington, D.C., Kolderie shared his thoughts on charter schools during an informal panel discussion that sought to assess the state of charter schools. Kolderie made it very clear that from his perspective, "there is no such thing as *a* charter school." Rather, he explained that charter schools were individual schools that reflected the innovation and inherent potential for success that, to him, naturally followed from the ability of schools to exist—in the thirty-seven states that had passed enabling legislation to then—outside of the "exclusive franchise" and the arguably crippling restrictions of the established public school bureaucracy.

The ideas of these three men, magnified by Minnesota's propensity for maverick social policy experiments, were embraced by education reformers of all stripes and political creeds and disseminated nationwide through a diverse network of political, academic, and educational leaders. Once Minnesota passed charter-enabling legislation in 1991, the idea had become a movement. This first law was soon followed by the creation of eight new schools, the first of which was City Academy in St. Paul, which opened its doors in 1992. After then, Minnesota's law was amended a number of times, and by fall 2001, an estimated 75 charter schools, serving approximately 9,600 students, were open for business.[18]

CITY ACADEMY: THE FIRST CHARTER SCHOOL

City Academy opened its doors in September 1992 to thirty-five middle and high school students who had chosen to join this fledgling experiment in educational reform. Operating in a city-owned building on the East Side of St. Paul, Minnesota, City Academy is situated in a neighborhood that was, and is, saddled with high poverty, unemployment, and high out-of-school rates. Most of the students who found their way to City Academy lived at or below the poverty level and arrived with a history of truancy and a feeling that they were too academically behind to succeed in the schools they had previously attended. Like many disadvantaged students, they had failed at school, just as surely as their schools had failed them. Nearly ten years later, City Academy is still going strong.

City Academy seeks to meet the academic and social needs of its students in a new way—with the idea that given a choice to attend a school that was designed specifically with them in mind, this population of students might be turned back on to education. Its founders wanted City Academy to be small, eventually limiting its enrollment to ninety students, thereby structurally guaranteeing small classes; it would be personal, with each student following an individually crafted learning plan and playing an active role in shaping the school's curriculum; and it would promote community, by providing opportunities for students to give back and giving parents multiple ways to become involved in the life of the school.

As a charter school, City Academy is a public school—but it operates independently of the local school district. It is exempt from all Minnesota statues and rules that govern "regular" public schools, though it must comply with all applicable state and federal health and safety regulations. Because City Academy is managed independently, its administration is responsible for coordinating not just its academic program and faculty, as is the case in most public schools, but also its physical plant and operations, food service, payroll and benefits, security, finances, and accounting. Under Minnesota law, City Academy is bound to an operating contract that defines the school's organizational and management structure, as well as its goals. This contract is issued by a state charter-sponsoring agency, in the case of City Academy, a local college. After ten years in operation and hundreds of students passing through its doors, City Academy has remained open—and it serves as a talisman for the entire charter school movement.

The 1990s

By the beginning of the 1990s, with the country heading for recession and a continuing sense that our students were not achieving at a rate commensurate with our status as a great nation, the problems of public education were, more than ever, being blamed on the system itself—the state and local governmental structures that had grown up and around public schools over the course of nearly a century. As had become common, international comparisons of test scores found American students far from the head of the class, just like in the early 1980s when *A Nation At Risk* was published. And consistently less-than-stellar results on domestic test scores did not make the situation any better. With such concentrated anger over the perceived state of American education, radical ideas had fertile ground in which to take root—especially ideas that targeted bloated government bureaucracy as the root of all evil, as the more radical flanks of the developing charter school movement did.

Those who viewed the system as the problem saw it as bloated and bureaucratic, beholden to political and union interests and therefore inefficient, unresponsive, and ineffective. From their perspective, years of "faddish" education reform movements had failed to make any substantial improvement in educational outcomes. In the words of one critic, "dumbed-down curricula, revisionist history, social promotion, 'new' math, whole-language reading, self-esteem quackery, and other destructive fads left far too many children intellectually handicapped for life."[19] Ironically enough, many of the charter schools that would open in the 1990s embraced these efforts as part of their innovative curricula–educational strategies that they claimed would promote student improvement and achievement. But those who were frustrated by years of failed educational reforms and enamored of new market policies of deregulation and small government saw these reform strategies as just one of many dragons to be slain—with the system itself the biggest dragon of them all.

Justified or not, new voices in education reform—armed with a new perspective on the appropriate role of government and little tolerance for the same old school-based reform strategies—began to emerge, spreading the gospel of new ideas and offering new assumptions upon which to build reform strategies and arguments. John Chubb and Terry Moe, two academics affiliated with the Brookings Institution and Stanford University, in their 1990 book *Politics, Markets and America's Schools*, were among the first to espouse a wholesale abandonment of school-centered reforms. Instead, they favored a new approach to school reform that would address external and systemic problems. Chubb and Moe wrote, "We believe existing institutions cannot solve the problem because they are the problem—and that the key to better schools is institutional reform."[20] Though Chubb and Moe do not explicitly promote or discuss the charter movement, they do believe that under their system, "Any group or organization that applies to the state and meets . . . minimal criteria must then be chartered as a public school and granted the right to accept students and receive public money."

Much of the charter movement is rooted in the same assumptions and philosophy that Chubb and Moe use to support their belief that the American public school system should be transformed into a market-based "economy" that forces autonomous, publicly funded schools to compete for students. Because the problems facing public schools are the direct result of their dependence on and connection to state and local boards of education, the most effective solution for these problems would be to create a new structure that would allow public schools to exist independently of these governmental agencies. Independence from bureaucracy and from its overbearing restrictions would allow schools the freedom to exist in their own image, educating students as they saw best, with their success (and survival) depending only on student performance. As long as students continued to demonstrate academic achievement, the school would continue to exist.

Chubb and Moe's ideas are, at first glance, without apparent ideology—and have appeal to radicals and conservatives alike. But beneath the surface, their quick-fix reform strategies reveal themselves as tools that when used have the potential to erode or even dismantle the assumptions upon which America's system of public education has traditionally been based.

By the end of 1996, twenty-seven charter laws were in effect nationwide. With the arrival of charter schools, the school choice and school voucher programs found renewed energy, introducing revolutionary—and to some, unconstitutional—ideas on how to reshape the face of American education. In September 1996, the conservative education expert Chester Finn was quoted in *The New York Times* as saying, "Over all, I think that we're moving toward a completely new strategy of delivering education that's not a top-down bureaucratically run approach, but a bottom-up grass roots approach."[21] The shift that Finn described would neatly set the stage for changing the existing system of government oversight and indirect control of public education to a market-based and market-driven system that would theoretically—eventually—

drive systemic educational improvement for all students through the magic of competition. In the same article, Lamar Alexander, former Tennessee governor and U.S. secretary of education, characterized the lack of school choice as "the Berlin Wall of domestic social policy." To conservatives, charter schools became a cause that was both innocent and subversive—it could be presented as a mainstream, common-sense idea for improving schools, increasing parental involvement and control over education, and eliminating government bureaucracy while at the same time be used as a symbol for all that was wrong with the public education system.

THE RISE OF FOR-PROFIT EDUCATION

Over the past ten years, for-profit companies have aggressively entered the K–12 educational marketplace. Indeed, revenues for K-12 and post-secondary sectors the education industry increased by an estimated 19% from 1998 to 2000, from $63.5 billion to $75.3 billion.[22]

Corporate involvement in education is not new. Publishing and media companies have been in the textbook, curriculum, and standardized test business for years. It is no longer uncommon for school districts to contract with food service companies to provide meals for students. Since the late 1980s, educational technology has become big business, especially since the Clinton administration passed E-Rate legislation in 1996, authorizing billions of dollars in federal grants and subsidies that would cover the cost of Internet connectivity and related equipment in public schools. Information technology companies, recognizing a cash cow that had just been born, began aggressively courting business from public schools districts.

What accounts for the tremendous increase in education-related business revenues over the course of just seven years? New ventures in for-profit professional development, teacher training, and school administration software; the establishment of for-profit educational management organizations (EMOs), an expansion in the scope and frequency of public school districts outsourcing essential services (such as security, cleaning and janitorial, food service, and information technology); new computer-based curricula and software—all fueled by the dot-com driven economic expansion of the mid- and late 1990s. Corporations are opening chains of charter schools, for-profit law schools, post-secondary institutions, and companies that provide continuing education to adults.

During the late 1990s, many major investment banks started following the education business, and a number of investment banking and venture capital firms, focusing exclusively or substantially on education-related investment opportunities, opened for business. A report from Montgomery Securities, as quoted by Corporate Watch in an online editorial, touts the education industry as ripe for investment: "The timing for entry into the education and training market has never been better. The problems with American education have elevated education reform to a high political priority and technology is demanding and enabling a transformation in the delivery of education."[23] Of course, in the aftermath of the dot-com bust and the burgeoning recession of 2001–2002, these industries, along with many others, are contracting. But the precedent has been set. In 2002, with the Edison Schools Corporation actively pursuing a contract to take over the management of many Philadelphia public schools, it is clear that while the growth of the education industry may be slowing down, it is not going to disappear.[24]

However, there is little evidence that privatization is doing a better job than the public sector—and there are many instances where privatization has actually done more harm than good. An excellent example of this can be found in Baltimore, which in 1992 turned the management of nine troubled schools over to Education Alternatives, Inc. (EAI), a publicly traded education management company. After four years of misrepresented test scores, inflated student attendance data, and violations of special education and Chapter 1 regulations, Baltimore terminated its contract with EAI.[25]

Edison's record as a private manager of public schools is less fraught with drama or fraud, but is equally mixed. Though Edison's own data consistently claims that students in its schools demonstrate substantial achievement gains and perform better than students in many comparable non-charter or privately held schools, outside analysis shows that these claims may not be as straightforward or airtight as Edison would have the public believe. Like any other public school, an Edison public school must confront the challenges of overcoming years of educational neglect that continues to affect the educational attitudes and aptitudes of so many under-served children.

With all of the enthusiasm for business involvement in a market-based education system, many people still have many concerns. Jonathan Kozol, noted educator and chronicler of urban public schools, asked for his thoughts on the decreasing confidence in public schools and services, replied, "We have to be careful not to succumb to this nonsense that a public system is inherently flawed and that there-fore we have to turn to the marketplace for solutions. I've never in my entire life seen any evidence that the competitive free market, unre-stricted, without a strong counterpoise within the public sector, will ever dispense decent medical care, sanitation, transportation, or educa-tion to the people."[26]

In the end, the rise of private involvement in public education ap-pears to be a trend that will not naturally reverse itself. What is not clear is how privatization will play out. Will the bulk of private compa-nies that are involved in education ventures focus on new education businesses, such as after-school student enrichment services, educa-tional software and resources for home use, and distance learning for adults, or will they increasingly focus on the wholesale takeover of public schools and districts? Today, private management companies operate approximately 300 public schools, out of more than 95,000 nationwide. Not even 10 percent of all charter schools are privately managed. So at least for the time being, the degree to which private in-dustry is involved in the core business of educating children is fairly limited. But as we have seen, EMOs continue to expand their reach seemingly without regard to whether or not they actually do a better job of educating children.

Nurturing the Movement: The Federal Influence

Not surprisingly, the Clinton administration began to actively em-brace charter schools early in its first administration—a perfect ex-ample of its "third way" strategy of adopting elements of more conservative policy in order to capture mainstream support and appeal to more liberal Republicans. It was also a strategy to divert support away from even more radical, predominantly Republicanchampioned proposals for school choice, including school vouchers and tuition tax-credits. These two movements were perceived as a far more dangerous assault on the American system of free, public, democratic education—and if it meant embracing charter schools to keep these two movements at bay, then so be it. Indeed, though these movements are still on the radar in 2002, they are far less front-and-center—and far less likely to be universally adopted—than they might have been had the Clinton administration and state legislatures across the country not adopted charter schools as a relatively innocuous compromise reform movement. The only group that remained consistently anti-charters throughout the 1990s was the nation's teachers unions. Even that resistance has receded over time, with some teachers unions going so far as to start their own charter schools as a way of demonstrating conditional acceptance of the movement. In 1999, Andrew Rotherham, director of the Progressive Policy Institute's Twenty-first Century Schools Project, articulated the "third way" approach to charter schools in testimony before a subcommittee of the House Committee on Education and the Workforce: "In short, PPI believes that a combination of private or market-based accountability and public accountability is the recipe for educational success. Parents should have choice and there should be competition within a public system, but taxpayers have a right to expect that their tax dollars are being invested in publicly accountable entities. Because they lack accountability for results, voucher proposals move away from greater accountability in education rather than reward it and don't define public outcomes of educational success."[27]

It was in 1993 that President Clinton first proposed a federal role in the charter school movement, proposing the Federal Charter School Program (FCSP). In 1994, the FCSP was enacted as Title X, Part C of the reauthorization of the Elementary and Secondary Education Act (ESEA).

The goal of the FCSP was to provide start-up and technical support for the creation of charter schools across the country. The act's initial appropriation was $5 million in the 1995 fiscal year, most of which was earmarked for charter school start-up costs that were, even then, recognized as among the toughest barriers to establishing charter schools. FCSP funds were, for the most part, funneled to schools through individual states.

Federal involvement in charter schools immediately changed the tenor of the movement, especially because accepting federal funding obligated charter schools to comply with all relevant federal rules and regulations, including civil rights legislation. Though some schools chose not to apply for or accept these monies, most charter schools did. The per pupil expenditure (PPE) for charter schools is generally less than the PPE for traditional public schools—by as much as 20 percent. This, plus the fact that many states do not provide funds for charter school facilities, means that charter schools need all the supplemental funding they can find.

The quid pro quo for accepting federal funds is that schools must be open to all students—no entrance examinations, screening, or other forms of selection permitted. At the beginning of the charter movement, many would-be charter operators saw an opportunity to create elite academies, paid for with public funds, that would cater to a specific sector of the student population. Some early charter schools required students to pass difficult entrance examinations or required parents to pledge many tens of hours of volunteer service in exchange for their child's admission. Other early charter schools opened without any provision for accommodating special education students or for adapting their curricula to children with different educational needs and abilities. With the introduction of federal funding, charter schools that had explicitly or implicitly designed educational programs that were not inclusive had to make a choice: accept much-needed federal funds and adapt their programs, or refuse these funds and make do with inadequate funding. Even this second option was not always viable, as some states began to question their legal ability to fund schools that in any way excluded certain groups of children and instead required charter schools to open their enrollment to any child who was interested in attending.

By the mid-1990s, the U.S. Department of Education began to actively court the charter school movement. Indeed, by initiating federal grant programs to support the development and implementation of charter schools across the country, the Department of Education was able to gain some degree of control over the charter school movement and to adopt a popular strategy that it could then claim responsibility—and take the credit—for.

By 1996, the Department of Education's role in the charter school movement had deepened. Staff was added to the Department's Office of Elementary and Secondary Programs to serve as a central resource point for the charter school program. Also in 1996, the Department allocated funds for a four-year comprehensive study of charter schools that would be conducted by outside evaluators. Soon, the Education Department was supporting an informational Web site on charter schools—www.uscharterschools.org—and began sponsoring national conferences on charter schools.

The FCSP was re-authorized in 1998 under the Charter Schools Expansion Act in response to President Clinton's call for 3,000 charter schools by the year 2000. The legislation also made explicit the fact that charter schools must have access to federal categorical funds such as Title I, special education, and bilingual education. By 2000, the federal appropriation for the FCSP grew to $145 million, with both new and established charter schools eligible for the funding.

In 2000, during a visit to St. Paul, Minnesota, President Clinton praised the charter movement—particularly the level of accountability that is found in good charter laws—while also criticizing some state charter laws, both for being too strict and too lax.[28] During a speech to students at the City Academy charter school, Clinton echoed the Progressive Policy Institute's middle-of-the-road policy: "Some states have laws that are so loose that no matter whether the charter schools are doing their job or not, they just get to stay open and they become like another bureaucracy. Even worse, some states have laws that are so restrictive it's almost impossible to open a charter school in the first place." He also praised the charter movement as a whole: "We now have enough evidence that the charter school movement works, if it's done right. Very often we see charter schools provide an even greater atmosphere of competition that induces kids to work harder and harder to learn."

By the end of 1999, all but one of the charter school laws in existence today had been passed. No laws were passed in 2000, and just one, Indiana, was passed in 2001. Though activists and supporters continued to push for the expansion of charters to the remaining twelve states, it is unclear whether this will happen. Many of the states where charters have not been adopted are not necessarily ready for this level of change, often because their population is not as widely dissatisfied with their system of public education as in states where charters were adopted more readily and more quickly. Even in states where the charter movement got off to an explosive start—in New York, for example, where nearly one hundred charter applications were submitted in the first months after the program was established, many of them ready even before the state had released official application documents—the movement has tempered somewhat. And it still remains the case that 52 percent (1,068 or 2,063) of all U.S. charter schools are located in just four states: Arizona, California, Michigan, and Texas. Though charters are a nationwide movement, their core is very localized.

In his 1999 State of the Union address[29], President Clinton called for 3,000 charters by the beginning of the twenty-first century, setting a bold numeric goal for the movement's growth—and for progress towards the systemic change that Clinton and the New Democrats promised would occur. By the time Clinton left office, however, the nation was nearly 1,000 schools short of that goal. The estimated number of charter schools open for business in September 2001 was 2,357—still short of the "goal" and representing just 2 percent of all U.S. public schools. Why is the movement coming up short?

By the closing days of the Clinton administration, some of the charter movement's rhetoric had begun to shift from a tone of exuberant boosterism and endless possibility to one that perhaps represented a movement that was beginning to get a taste of cold reality. Charter supporters began espousing a strident "us versus them" philosophy, and exhorting "real charter supporters to beware of coming threats to their freedom and independence."

Charter Schools Today: Into the New Millennium

Though charters are not as front-and-center a reform issue for the Bush administration as for the Clinton, the new administration does support the movement. Charter schools continue to be a middle-of-the road reform strategy that is embraced by both sides because of its essential status as an "empty vessel,"[30] into which almost any ideology can be placed and from which reform strategies to suit any political outlook can be poured. Given the movement's status as a high-profile movement that actually involves a low number of schools, what does the future hold?

Within states that already permit charter schools, there is an ongoing legislative dance between pro- and anti-charter forces—resulting in legislation that is often under revision. The politics of amending charter laws usually involves conflicting efforts to make the law weaker (making it harder for charters to operate) or stronger (attempting to legislatively ease barriers to charter schools such as facilities or transportation issues.) So while the movement may very well have reached its upper limit of the number of states that will be involved, the movement has not stopped trying to reinvent itself, to make it easier to open and sustain charter schools.

Does this rollback and redirection of legislative activity mean the movement is over? We don't think so. But it may mean that the movement is reaching maturity and that the honeymoon period is over. Today, many charter schools have been in operation for at least eight years, and hundreds more are at least five years old. Many charters have already been up for renewal, and most have been renewed. Claims are still made that charter schools will catalyze widespread change in American public education, but the state of our schools is still of concern. The charter movement has developed a powerful support network for parents, teachers, and communities involved in charter schools—thanks equally to the Internet and to the tireless efforts of charter movement leaders like Joe Nathan and Jeanne Allen—but it has not yet extended that network, for the most part, into the traditional system. Within the

movement, people share strategies for everything from finding facilities to fighting state education department bureaucracy. But
they do not often make the effort to share their lessons learned
with the broader public education community. Charter schools are
an exclusive club of enlightened education professionals. To share
their trade secrets might, in the long run, jeopardize their very existence.

This burgeoning "us-versus-them" mindset was present at the
2000 National Charter School Conference, held in Washington,
D.C., in December 2000. Twenty months had passed since the previous National Charter School Conference, which took place in
March 1999 in Denver. In the intervening time period, much had
changed: George W. Bush was about to be inaugurated as the
forty-third president of the United States; the economy was contracting; and the financial exuberance and optimism of the dot-
com era had given way to a more reserved and markedly less lucra-
tive reality. Charter schools reached their peak popularity during
the same late-1990s years that Internet entreprenurism was at its
most popular and was inspiring millions of Americans to join the
party by investing in the stock market at previously unheard-of
levels and to value private initiative over public service. When the
bubble burst, so did some of the exuberance that had fueled the
movement's initial fire.

At the 1999 conference, the prevailing attitude among partici-
pants was one of unlimited possibility, with a maverick spirit in
the air. The attitude at the 2000 conference was more cautious,
with people explicitly warning charter school proponents to be
vigilant against all those who would take the movement away from
them. In the words of Steve Overton, who founded a Michigan
charter school and who is an active voice in the national conversa-
tion about charter schools, "The movement is 'stalled,' and the
only way to keep it alive is for its supporters to adopt a 'revolutionary' mentality—to keep from being 'killed.'"[31] With a sense
that the movement was no longer sweeping the nation, it seemed
that the prevailing attitude was to celebrate successes to date
while strategizing for long-term survival.

In March 2001, U.S. Senator Tom Carper, a Democrat of Delaware, introduced a bipartisan education bill—co-sponsored with Senator Judd Gregg, a Republican of New Hampshire—entitled the Empowering Parents Act. This bill sought to enhance the viability of charter schools across the country by allocating federal funds to support charter schools in two areas that consistently present challenges: a lack of capital funds and the fact that they typically receive less funding, per student, than do regular public schools. The bill proposed a yearly $400 million guaranteed loan program for charter schools to help fund capital needs; an additional $200 million in grants to states to help states direct the same amount of per capita funding to charter schools as they do to traditional public schools; and a $200 million annual fund that would be used to encourage public school choice and charter schools in the nation's poorest school districts.[32]

In October 2001, the Bush administration's secretary of education, the former Houston Schools Superintendent Roderick C. Paige, announced $182 million in federal funds for charter schools to support "expanded options for parents and children in nineteen states, Washington, D.C., and Puerto Rico."[33] The money would "go to help set up, develop, and expand charter schools and to promote the exchange of information regarding what works to improve student performance among charter schools across the nation." Most of this money is to be awarded in the form of three-year grants to individual states, which, in turn, are to award the money to schools in the form of start-up and other grants. Arizona is the exception—with money going directly to sixty-five charter schools and bypassing the Arizona State Department of Education. An additional $7 million from the federal allocation is to be used to support "field-initiated national activities including research and data collection, technical assistance, providing information on facilities, and sharing best practices in instruction and assessment."

In the final analysis, $182 million represents a small percentage of the amount of money that is spent on education and related services in this country in any given year (2000 estimated federal expenditure on public education: $350 billion)—but it does represent the Bush administration's continued support of the program. Indeed, the President's proposed budget for 2003 includes $200 million for the charter schools program—a small increase over current funding levels. The U.S. Department of Education continues to support the charter movement and will host the fourth National Charter Schools Conference in Milwaukee in June 2002. But the degree to which charter schools will define—or be defined by— the Bush administration's education policy is unclear.

With fall 2001 economic indicators showing a protracted recession, with the federal surplus having been spent down following the Bush tax refund plan of 2001, with new federal emphasis on standards and testing, with decreased federal revenues—and now in the aftermath of the tragic events of September 11, 2001, and the economic ripple effects that are already being seen—it is unlikely that the federal government will be able to support the wholesale expansion of charters in any meaningful financial way for at least the immediate future. Though charters can survive without federal funding—all it takes is a state enabling law—state and local education priorities are often determined the old-fashioned way: the action is where the money is. So it remains to be seen what happens to the movement in the years to come. Will the movement stop expanding but continue to grow in the states where it has already laid down roots, or will it begin to contract, in the face of other, more urgent, local and national priorities?

CHARTER SCHOOL LEGISLATION: A PRIMER

Though the U.S. Department of Education actively supports the charter movement through grant programs, research and evaluation studies, and professional development and support—and though the U.S. government supports the creation and growth of the charter movement by providing a variety of monies to support charter schools at the local and state level—the federal government cannot require states to ratify charter legislation. Public education is a domain over which the states preside. As with nearly all aspects of public education in the United States, the decision whether or not to allow charter schools is made on a state-by-state basis.

Charter school legislation is on the books in thirty-seven states and the District of Columbia; charter schools operate in all but three of these locations (Indiana, New Hampshire, and Wyoming). This means that there are thirty-five distinct environments under which charter schools operate and under which the movement grows and develops. Though each law is different, all charter laws, on a basic level, follow Ted Kolderie's blueprint for empowering and enabling nongovernmental entities to propose school designs that may, if approved by a state's designated chartering entity, receive public funds in support of their school.

Despite the differences among laws, there are enough common legislative components to enable us to compare and contrast laws and place them on a continuum that stretches from "strong" laws (those that promote the establishment of charter schools) to "weak" laws (those that discourage the establishment of charter schools).

As defined by the Center for Education Reform (CER), strong charter laws:

- Place few restrictions on the number of charter schools allowed;
- Authorize multiple chartering entities;
- Allow a wide range of individuals and groups to apply for and receive charters;
- Permit new and conversion charter schools;
- Do not require charter applicants to demonstrate strong community support prior to the granting of a charter;
- Automatically waive most or all state and local education laws, regulations, and policies;
- Grant charter schools high degrees of legal and operational autonomy;
- Guarantee that 100 percent of per-pupil funding flows to charter schools;
- Grant schools fiscal autonomy;
- Exempt charter schools from collective bargaining agreements and district work rules.

Weak charter laws:

- Place restrictions on the number of charter schools allowed;
- Authorize a single chartering entity;

- Restrict the types of individuals or groups that may apply for and receive charters;
- Permit only conversion schools;
- Require charter applicants to demonstrate strong community support prior to the granting of a charter;
- Do not automatically waive state and local education laws, regulations, and policies;
- Restrict charter schools' legal and operational autonomy;
- Do not guarantee that 100 percent of per-pupil funding flows to charter schools;
- Do not grant charter schools fiscal autonomy;
- Do not exempt charter schools from collective bargaining agreements and district work rules.[34]

In practice, each charter law occupies a place somewhere between the poles of strong and weak. The Center for Education Reform, a leading advocate for the charter school movement, releases an annual ranking of state charter school laws based on how each state's charter law measures up to the center's criteria. According to its November 2001 assessment, the thirty-eight charter laws rank, from strongest to weakest, as follows:[35]

1.	Arizona	20.	New Mexico
2.	Delaware	21.	Illinois
3.	Minnesota	22.	Georgia
4.	Washington, D.C.	23.	Oklahoma
5.	Michigan	24.	South Carolina
6.	Indiana	25.	Louisiana
7.	Massachusetts	26.	Idaho
8.	Florida	27.	Connecticut
9.	Colorado	28.	Nevada
10.	New York	29.	Utah
11.	California	30.	Wyoming
12.	North Carolina	31.	New Hampshire
13.	Pennsylvania	32.	Alaska
14.	Ohio	33.	Hawaii
15.	Missouri	34.	Arkansas
16.	Oregon	35.	Rhode Island
17.	New Jersey	36.	Virginia
18.	Wisconsin	37.	Kansas
19.	Texas	38.	Mississippi

HOW CHARTER SCHOOLS WORK

Frequently Asked Questions

With so much publicity around the charter movement, and with so much variability between and among charter laws and the schools they enable, it is difficult to characterize charter schools in simple or consistent terms. It's often difficult to even answer a simple question about charter schools—for example, what entity is authorized to grant charters—because the answer varies from state to state. However, it is possible to provide general answers to general questions. In this next section, we will pose and answer some key questions about charter schools.

1. Who can start a charter school?

Depending on the specific law of each state, charters may be started by individuals, including parents, teachers, and community representatives; nonprofit or community-based organizations; for-profit corporations; museums or cultural institutions; and nonprofit, non-sectarian arms of religious institutions—or by any combination of the above. Most U.S. charter schools, to date, were created as new schools—80 percent, in fact—and were started by individuals or coalitions of people who decided that they have what it takes to establish and run a successful school.[36] The remaining 20 percent of charter schools converted from traditional public schools (or, in some states, from private schools) to charter status.

Charter schools can elect to develop their own curricula and educational programs to reflect their unique visions or to purchase ready-made curricula that reflect a desired educational approach. Charter schools can build an operating budget based on the assumption that their only source of revenue will be state-provided per-pupil expenditure (PPE) funds, or they can elect to seek external funding to cover the costs of everything and anything from facilities to faculty. Charter schools can choose to partner with local businesses, cultural institutions, universities, or nonprofit organizations—or not. Charter schools can choose to outsource non-academic functions like school security, food service, benefits administration, and technology—or they can choose to manage all of these functions themselves. Charter schools can follow traditional grade configurations and scheduling plans or create their own.

In short, charter schools can create themselves in their own image. If the organizers of a prospective charter school demonstrate in their charter application that their definition of their educational plan is likely to result in high student achievement as defined by the percentage of students who will meet or exceed state standards, then their application has a good chance of being successful. And with an approved charter in hand, the process of actually turning their vision into reality can begin.

2. What does a charter application look like?

Charter applications vary dramatically by state, though they all share one key characteristic: They take a lot of time to complete and ask for a lot of detailed information. In general, charter school applications require the person or entity that is proposing the charter to answer a lengthy series of questions about the school's educational vision, proposed instructional design and faculty, budget and facility plans, and proposed accountability and measurements of school success. For a sample state charter application (New York), please see the Appendix.

3. How do charters get awarded?

After a charter application is completed, and multiple copies of this long and detailed document are submitted to a state chartering agency, it generally takes a few months for prospective charter operators to receive a decision on their application. As mentioned above, a successful application must make a strong and convincing case that the proposed school design has merit, that the proposed leadership team and administrators have the experience and ability to actually run a school, that the proposed school's performance and accountability goals seem realistic and reachable, and that the school's operating budget has been developed prudently and responsibly. In most states, particularly in those with few or no restrictions on the number of charter schools that may open, a solid application has a good chance of being approved.

In some states, charter applications are subject to rigorous scrutiny;[37] in others, charters are approved much more easily. Some states, like Mississippi, have a single chartering entity that reviews and grants charters; others, including New York, Arizona, and Michigan, present prospective charter operators with a choice of where to submit their charter application. When there is a choice, decisions are often made based on the answer to the question: "Which chartering entity will give me the most freedom with the least oversight?" In states like Michigan and Arizona, there may be an advantage to applying to a district, rather than the state chartering agency—as districts can award charters to schools that will operate thousands of miles away from their central office—so as to avoid unnecessary entanglements and hands-on oversight. In New York, which has three chartering entities, many would-be operators of charter schools in New York City apply directly to the State University of New York rather than to the New York City Board of Education (itself a chartering entity) in order to put as much distance as possible between the New York City school system (which is perceived by many to be a bureaucratic nightmare) and the applicant's efforts to create an independent school.

4. How are charter schools funded?

Charter schools generally receive a fixed per-pupil dollar amount from the state that is usually less than what is budgeted for per-pupil expenditures (PPEs) at traditional public schools. This discrepancy is generally attributable to the fact that charter schools, as stand-alone entities, do not use district services, services that are paid for through the regular per-pupil expenditures. However, this discrepancy forms the basis of one of the biggest challenges that face charter schools: lack of adequate operating funds. While it is true that charter schools are generally able to support basic academic and instructional support programs using the PPE revenue they receive from the state, it is equally true that "the basics" are all that they can provide. Many charter schools find themselves unable to pay for after-school activities, sports, or extra-curricular clubs; unable to fund arts, music, or theater programs; and unable to create adequate libraries, science facilities, or computer labs. This raises the question of whether charter schools can actually provide as robust an educational experience for children as can many traditional public schools. Some charter school advocates even see this discrepancy as evidence that the system doesn't want charter schools to succeed—because funding policy does nothing to provide a level playing field between charters and traditional public schools.

All that being said, charter schools do have other options for obtaining funds and other potential revenue sources. Charter schools are eligible to apply for federal categorical aid monies—including Title I funding and funding for special education and bilingual education. Charter schools often look to nongovernmental sources for other types of revenue, to help fulfill the promise of a more enriching and supportive educational environment for the children they serve. Charter schools that actively seek external funding—including foundation grants, corporate support, and in-kind donations of facilities, services, or infrastructure—are different from schools that choose not to. Clearly, external support plays a critical role in allowing schools to offer more services and to stabilize during periods of financial uncertainty. In the case of charter schools operated by Education Management Organizations, additional resources flow as a result of economies of scale, corporate profits, and capital dollars that are invested for eventual return as profit to shareholders.

5. What kind of relationship do charter schools have with their local districts?

How charter schools operate in the context of the larger public school system also varies by state, and even more so by district.

Some school districts have come to embrace charters, some going as far as to try to define themselves as charter districts; others treat charter schools as mortal enemies, providing no support or camaraderie whatsoever. Some school districts provide new charter schools with facilities and access to administrative infrastructure; others leave charter schools to fend for themselves. Some school districts are generous in their efforts to share transportation resources, in some cases even including charter schools and their students on their school bus routes; other school districts do nothing to help students travel to and from charter schools. Some districts share professional development opportunities with teachers in charter schools; others don't. In theory, a major component of the charter school movement is the promise that there will be an active transfer of ideas and best practices between charter schools and traditional public schools. But in practice, it is not clear that this is happening very much, if at all. Charter school teachers and administrators are often too busy and too overworked to make an effort to share their programs and practices with others—especially with others who, in fact, work for the competition.

6. Who provides infrastructure services like security, technology and food service?

Because charter schools operate without the support of local school districts and established support networks, school leadership is responsible not only for all the usual issues of school administration but also for infrastructure and facilities management. This means finding vendors for payroll and benefits; locating and in some cases renovating space for the schools; hiring and supervising cafeteria and security staff; identifying and selecting vendors to provide computers and other technology; and managing the school's physical plant and supervising custodial and janitorial staff. Some schools choose to manage all of these areas in-house. Others outsource many, if not all, non-educational functions. Yet others make arrangements with their former or local school district to provide (for a fee) food service, security, and payroll. As it is, the job of a school principal or director is over-whelming; at a charter school it can be nearly impossible—espe-cially since most principals, while they may have considerable ex-perience as educators, have little experience as facilities managers or chief operating officers.

7. How does a child become eligible to enroll in a charter school?

Theoretically, any child is eligible to attend any local charter school, as long as there is room for him or her. In some states, fami-lies are theoretically free to send their child to any charter school. Still other states have authorized charter schools that support home-schooled children—meaning that there is no central school location at all. Most charter schools must, according to state law, admit any student who applies; admissions testing or other selec-tion criteria are looked upon as potentially discriminating and re-strictive. Charter school enrollment, therefore, is generally done on a first-come, first-serve basis. According to the Center for Educa-tion Reform, 75 percent of charter schools surveyed reported that they had a waiting list of students for their school.[38]

Not all charter schools started out with arms open wide to any-one. During the movement's early years, some charter schools were founded specifically to provide educational havens for gifted chil-dren, special needs children, or children with disabilities. Schools defended this practice, arguing that charter schools exist to pro-vide parents and communities with new educational options. In ad-dition, not all charter schools developed facilities or instructional plans that would accommodate children of different skill or ability levels. As the years passed, however, and particularly as the federal government got involved in supporting the charter movement, more explicit rules were written. It became clear that, for a charter school to receive any federal funds, it had to comply with federal civil rights and ADA laws. Moreover, it often became easier to sell the charter concept if it could be demonstrated that charter schools were open to the same population of students as were traditional public schools. In short, opening the doors of charter schools to everyone made it difficult for opponents to accuse charter schools of "creaming" the best students from the population at large.

Some charter schools define their educational mission so narrowly that only a special segment of students could meaningfully apply. Schools that cater to deaf or hard-of-hearing students, for example, are not likely to hold that much interest for parents with children who hear normally. Schools that emphasize experiential and outdoor education are not likely to attract children who hate the outdoors or who are not athletic. Schools that specifically cater to "at-risk" populations are not likely to appeal to parents of children who are not at risk. As long as charter schools do not explicitly discriminate, they are in compliance with the law—but by narrowly defining their niches, many charter schools *de facto* restrict their student body.

8. How are charter schools held accountable?

Charter schools are supposed to be held to the highest standard of accountability. A school must meet the accountability and student achievement goals it outlines in its charter and its students must perform well on the same state-administered standardized tests that children at traditional public schools take. If a charter school doesn't meet its goals, it risks losing its charter and being forced to close its doors. This seemingly straightforward policy, which provides clear and theoretically air-tight direction as to when a charter school can be closed, is, in fact, much less clear and much more complicated in practice—not unlike the accountability dilemma that faces most traditional public schools.

In 1996, during the heyday of the charter movement's growth, Joe Nathan, director of the Center for School Change at the University of Minnesota and a vocal supporter of the charter idea, recognized the critical need for clearly articulated accountability goals and measures that would be agreed upon by both the state chartering entity and a given charter school.[39] This two-way clarity and accountability is, theoretically, part of every charter application, but in practice, fuzzy or unrealistic accountability goals set by would-be charter operators are accepted every day. And states sometimes find themselves unable to actually implement charter school accountability safeguards, which means that charters get reviewed and in some cases renewed without actually facing a strict accountability review, not unlike the thousands of other public schools in the United States.

A 1998 report issued by the University of Minnesota's Center for School Change, a stalwart champion of the charter school movement, called upon charter sponsors and operators to be exceedingly clear about several critical issues, including measurable goals, assessments, and acceptable levels of student performance. Nathan, one of the report's authors, acknowledged that the degree to which this is actually happening at charter schools nationwide is mixed, despite the fact that all charter-enabling legislation is based on the assumption that charter schools are held to a higher standard of accountability than other public schools.[40] As eloquently stated by Kate Zernike in a March 2001 essay in *The New York Times*, "Ultimately, it is in the charter schools' interest to develop specific measures of success and failure. This might allow states to begin shutting them down, which paradoxically, might indicate that the movement has begun working as it should."[41]

9. For how long can a charter school operate? How are charters renewed?

The number of years that charters are authorized for varies by state. The duration of initial charters ranges from three years (Arkansas, Minnesota) to five years (New York, Colorado) to fifteen years (Arizona). Most state laws indicate that as long as a charter school meets the performance goals outlined in its original contract, and as long as the school or its administration does not do anything illegal or fraudulent, the charter will be renewed. In short, despite the fact that one of the strongest rationales behind the charter idea is that it would bring strict ac-

State	Number of charter schools operating as of 12/00	Number of schools closed as of 12/00
Alaska	18	1
Arizona	451	21
California	282	6
Colorado	82	2
Connecticut	17	1
Delaware	8	1
District of Columbia	40	2
Florida	160	7
Illinois	24	1
Massachusetts	43	2
Michigan	191	6
Minnesota	74	6
Nevada	8	1
New Jersey	57	2
North Carolina	98	8
Ohio	72	2
Oklahoma	7	1
Pennsylvania	66	1
South Carolina	11	3
Texas	169	10
Wisconsin	91	2
Totals	1969	86

Source: Center for Education Reform

The number of charter schools that have closed, by state, as of December 2000.

countability into the public school system, accountability is not strict at all. Why? Because as in all public schools, student performance indicators—upon which most charter school performance goals are based—are open to broad interpretation.

The truth is that not many charter schools have shut their doors. As of December 2000, just eighty-six charter schools—

representing approximately 4 percent of the total number of charter schools open during the 2000–01 school year—had closed. Half of the charters that have closed are located in four states: Arizona, California, Michigan, and Texas. This is not surprising, since these are the states with the most charter schools. Almost all charter schools have been closed for financial, not academic, reasons. Assuming that a charter operator has not done anything illegal, and that student test scores haven't radically fallen, there are very few reasons for a state chartering entity not to renew a charter.

The Center for Education Reform, a Washington, D.C.-based advocacy and research organization that energetically supports charter schools and market-based educational reform initiatives, claims that even this relatively small number of charter closings is a triumph, as it has historically been nearly impossible to close a failing traditional public school. Perhaps this small number of closings is actually due to the fact that the theory of strict, contractual charter school accountability is just that—a theory that has yet to be consistently transformed into practice.

TURNING DREAMS INTO REALITY:
BUILDING A CHARTER SCHOOL

Creating a new charter school, or converting an existing public or private school to charter status, is neither easy nor quick, no matter in what state a prospective charter operator is located. It is a multi-year, potentially high-risk undertaking that resembles nothing so much as the process of launching a start-up business. Depending on the politics of the state and/or the local community, this process can be easy and quick or long and drawn out. And the amount of ongoing support that a charter school gets depends greatly on how supportive the state and local community is to the charter idea. Charter-friendly states or districts often go out of their way to help charter schools find facilities and to provide start-up grants; charter-unfriendly states or districts sometimes make it exceedingly difficult for charters to get started, by bringing lawsuits, withholding transportation, or worse.

To get a feeling for what it is like to start a charter school, we will now take you through the process step by step. We start by creating a fictional, but typical, charter school founder: Mary Smith, a veteran teacher who is looking for a way to realize her educational vision but who has chosen not to pursue a traditional career path by becoming a public school principal. She believes that the existing school bureaucracy in her state and community is a roadblock to educational innovation and that the only way to realize her educational vision is to strike out on her own. Mary's story is not uncommon—in fact, according to the U.S. Department of Education, it is the story of the vast majority (70 percent) of charter school founders. Mary wants to start a school in the same district where she currently teaches, a midsized city with many affluent suburbs but a relatively depressed downtown residential area. She hopes that her school will be attractive to parents from both areas and will serve a student population that is both socioeconomically and ethnically diverse.

Mary's strength is that she is an experienced, respected elementary school teacher who has successfully developed engaging and innovative curricula, especially in the areas of social studies and language arts. Mary has no formal business or administrative experience, though she has effectively headed a number of teacher committees and is active in a number of other community organizations, including the PTA of a nearby middle school. Mary's weaknesses are common to many who decide to start a charter school: no experience in business, facilities management, or school administration; no experience hiring or firing staff; no experience with accounting, grants administration, or bookkeeping; no expertise in other key curriculum areas such as math, science, and physical education; no experience with special education or disabled students. Clearly, Mary is going to need help if she is going to succeed.

To succeed, Mary must go through a lengthy process, one that requires perseverance and a little guile. We have divided this process into five phases, and in the pages to follow, will examine the choices and challenges that Mary faces at each step of the way.

Phase I: Defining an Educational Vision

Before Mary begins work on her charter application, she's got a lot of decisions to make—decisions that will impact the entire future of her charter school dream.

New or Conversion?

Mary must decide whether to convert an existing public or private school to charter status or to build a new charter school. If she decides to take the conversion route, she will likely need to present her plan to the school community—especially the parents and faculty—and be able to garner the support of at least 50 percent of this community in a formal vote. If Mary decides to form a new school, she does not have to demonstrate community support—though she may be asked to demonstrate community need in her application to justify the creation of a new school.

Selecting Partners—or Going it Alone?

Once established, charter schools are generally considered to be autonomous institutions, with fiscal and legal autonomy. But it often helps to have an experienced partner—perhaps an existing nonprofit or community-based organization—to help shape the development process and to provide guidance and institutional support. Mary must decide if she wants to establish a new supporting organization or to affiliate with an existing organization.

To EMO or not to EMO?

Another critical decision for Mary: whether or not to contract with an Education Management Organization (EMO), which would step in and run her charter school. On the upside, this would relieve Mary of many, if not all, of the responsibilities of creating a charter school—because most EMOs are in the business of replication and scale, developing curricula, creating management structures, offering professional development, and providing non-instructional services. However, it would be unlikely that Mary would be able to remain in a leadership role at the charter school she wanted to create, as most EMOs also bring in their own administrators and, where permissible, their own faculty. And it would be more than likely that Mary would have no input on the school's curriculum or educational vision, as most EMO chains utilize a standard curricula at every site they operate. Of course, EMOs allow for some degree of local customization, but that's a far cry from realizing a personal educational vision. Currently, slightly fewer than 10 percent of all charter schools are run by for-profit EMOs.

Defining and Refining an Educational Vision.
Mary also needs to begin defining what her school is going to look like. She'll probably start by making a list of all the things that will be different about her school—all the things that will make her school better and more effective than all the other public schools where she or her fellow teachers have ever taught.

Also important: selecting a name for her school. Charter schools, in essence, are small businesses that must attract customers—students—so having a catchy name is often of great value. Of course, the trick is to have both an attractive name and a meaningful educational program—developing that is a task that will fall to Mary and her team in the months ahead. What name has Mary selected for her school? The Children Are Really Excellent Academy—the CARE Academy, for short.

Early Public Relations.
Now that she's getting close to being able to describe the CARE Academy's vision and explain how it is going to meet unmet community needs and provide an excellent education for all who attend it, Mary should begin building community support. She might want to reach out to local parents—future customers. She might want to reach out to local businesspeople to explain her

school's vision and enlist their support for in-kind resources and as a source of volunteers for the after-school tutoring program she is going to build into her charter school's budget. She might want to reach out to local elected officials, to let them know that a charter might be coming to their neighborhood—and to enlist their support should any negative legislation be floated. She might want to court the press. And she might want to reach out to the local teachers union. If she's in a state where collective bargaining agreements are not in effect for new charter schools, it's a good bet that local teachers unions are not going to be big fans of charter schools. But you never know. Teachers union positions on charter schools run the gamut, and in the interest of the children she will serve and the teachers she will need to recruit, it's worth it to try to bring the union on as an ally.

Phase II: Developing and Submitting a Charter Application

With Phase I completed, Mary's got her ideas set and her partners confirmed. Now, she must package her vision into a successful charter application, which will take time, energy, community support—and money.

Obtaining Seed Support.
It's a good bet that the process of developing her charter vision and team—in preparation for the task of completing and submitting a solid application to one of her state's chartering entities—is taking up most of Mary's time. If she's partnering with a community-based organization, which is likely, agency staff are most probably spending a substantial amount of time on this project as well. And time equals money. If Mary is lucky, she lives in a state that administers a seed grant program that will provide funds—in some cases, up to $50,000 or more—to help pay for costs associated with developing a charter application, including consultant fees (to curriculum designers), professional fees (to attorneys helping to structure the board of directors and establish legal autonomy), and perhaps even to Mary for her time. The federal govern-

ment funds a large portion of this program through block grants to state departments of education; in some cases, prospective charter school operators may be able to apply directly to the federal government for seed funding.

Mary can also approach private funders—individuals, foundations, corporations—and ask for their partnership and seed support of her charter vision. Since Mary is affiliated with a nonprofit organization, these donations may be tax-deductible, as are other in-kind services Mary might be able to obtain, such as office space, professional advice, and—if Mary is very lucky—space for her school.

Choosing Curricula, Pedagogy, and an Educational Philosophy.
What does the CARE Academy stand for? What are its educational and social values? Mary will have to be able to clearly articulate her school's vision and the pedagogical strategies she will employ to reach it. What grades will her school serve? Will the school day be traditionally structured or will she employ an innovative design to complement a new approach to teaching? Will her school have a special theme? Will it focus on basics or will it take a more progressive approach? What curricula will she use—an off-the-shelf program, which she would purchase from a curriculum company, or a curriculum of her and her team's own design? What textbooks and educational materials will she use? How will she integrate technology into the classroom and the educational atmosphere? What kind of ongoing professional development programs will she have for her faculty? And last, but perhaps most importantly, how will she integrate student evaluation into her school program—in order to demonstrate student performance and achievement. All of these decisions have financial and staffing implications. The sooner Mary figures out what her school is going to look like, the sooner she can craft a budget, build an administrative structure, and figure out how to get the resources she needs.

Does Anyone Have an Extra Building?
The problems of finding suitable facilities, and obtaining capital funds that can be used to lease, buy, or build space, are consistently ranked as the top challenges facing would-be charter

schools.[42] Mary has a number of options: finding unused space in a local school or school building (though this depends entirely on how amenable the local district is to charter schools; some district's won't provide space out of fear of competition); sharing space with one of her nonprofit partners, such as a community-based organization, a museum, a corporation, or a local university or community college; finding suitable space to rent. If Mary is very lucky, she will have a benefactor who will enable her to buy or build a building.

Some states do have grant programs that provide capital funds to qualified applicants. However, these funds tend to be limited. Increasingly, as policymakers and state legislators realize how prohibitive the facilities barrier is to charter schools, some states, such as Arizona, are adopting innovative strategies for funding charter school buildings, such as allowing charter schools to partner with local entities authorized to issue debt in the form of bonds—which, in turn, lend the proceeds to the school.

Writing the Application.
As described in the previous section, writing a charter application is a time-consuming undertaking that requires the applicant to provide vast amounts of detailed information that will help the chartering agency determine whether or not the proposed charter school seems viable and worthwhile. The charter application that Mary and her team ultimately submit to the chartering entity of their choice will, upon approval, serve as a blueprint for creating and running the school. Writing a powerful charter application will make the process of launching the school more straightforward, though not necessarily easier.

What components of a charter application are most important, both to the chartering entity and to the charter school itself?

- A well-written mission statement will demonstrate clarity of purpose.
- A clearly articulated educational program and a well-defined pedagogical model will help to ensure focus and to hire appropriately experienced faculty and staff.

- A plan for how the school will serve special needs students will demonstrate preparedness for the range of students that may choose to attend their school.
- A well thought-out and comprehensive student evaluation plan will pave the way for a straightforward accountability relationship with the state department of education and the chartering agency.
- A facility already lined up will demonstrate commitment and the ability of the charter school's leadership team to secure infrastructure.
- A workable marketing plan will help convince the chartering agency that the charter will be able to attract and enroll enough students to balance the yearly budget.
- A sound and thorough budget will demonstrate fiscal responsibility.
- An efficient and effective governance and management structure will signal that the charter school's founders have thought seriously about the human resources necessary to make the school work—and about how to structure the chain of command to promote a vibrant and effective educational institution.
- A comprehensive plan for parental involvement will show that the school has community support.
- A detailed human resources plan that provides assurances that the school will be able to meet all legal criteria, including federal civil rights and equal-access laws, will indicate the school's willingness to follow and support all applicable state and federal rules and regulations.

Building a Budget.

Creating a workable budget for a charter school is, indeed, one of the toughest challenges that a charter school founder or founding coalition faces. In the absence of outside funds, such as private grants or federal categorical aid, a charter school's revenue stream is quite straightforward: the number of students times a fixed per-pupil amount that is determined by the state legislature. If Mary's school plans to enroll 100 students in year one, and the state per-pupil allocation for elementary school students (the grade level she has chosen for her school) is $5,500, Mary's starting budget—for everything from facilities to teacher salaries, from security services to computer systems, from textbooks to chalk—is $550,000.

Depending on her population, Mary may be able to apply for federal aid—if she finds herself serving a population that is heavily low income, she will be able to apply for Title I funding as well as funding to pay for the cost of free or reduced price lunch programs. Mary is also free to seek outside funding to cover projected shortfalls and to build relationships with corporations or other outside groups to provide donations of equipment, supplies, and more.

Setting Accountability Goals.
The key to the entire charter concept is accountability—in exchange for freedom from bureaucracy and "the system," charter schools agree to be held strictly accountable for student performance and educational achievement. However, this strict accountability—and the process of strictly defining how and when students and schools will be evaluated—is to this day a core weakness of many charter laws.

All charter laws ask schools to explicitly state performance goals and to explain how they will measure progress toward goals. And, almost all charter laws require charter students to take all the same state-administered standardized tests as do students in traditional public schools. But the mechanics of interpreting this data and determining whether a school has met its goals and is performing adequately as compared to non-charter schools are shaky and inconsistent at best. In the end, as with all public schools, there are mitigating factors affecting school and student performance data that are impossible to envision when a charter is first starting out. For example, the CARE Academy might define its accountability goals in terms of a percentage of students scoring above a certain percentile—perhaps the seventieth—on a particular state test. Once Mary's charter is approved, she's got a defined accountability goal. But what happens if the state changes the standardized test? Or adopts new proficiency or content standards? Or what happens if the student population at Mary's school ends up being different than she expected—a population that is much further behind in terms of performance and academic ability than the population she had in mind when she planned her accountability goals?

In the end, Mary and the CARE Academy would, if necessary, address changes to their situation by seeking to re-define accountability goals. But in doing so, they are tweaking the original premise of strict accountability, by changing the rules and the goals midstream, and they are necessarily begging the question: if charter schools can change their accountability plans midstream, how will they ever be held truly accountable and what makes them different from traditional public schools?

To Which Chartering Agency Should We Submit our Application?
Depending in which state Mary is located, she may have many—or few—choices as to where to submit her charter school application. Some states, like Mississippi, have a single entity to which to submit a charter application, the local school board. Other states, like Michigan and Arizona, have a wide range of choices, including any school district in the state, a specially created state chartering authority, public institutions of higher education, or the state board of education itself. There is strategy involved in the choice, strategies that shift from state to state. In the end, the decision as to where to submit a charter application rests on the answer to this question: Which chartering entity will provide me with the most support, the most freedom, and the least red tape?

Phase III: From Approval to Opening

With charter in hand, the next few months are going to be busy ones for Mary and her team. Over the next six months, Mary will have to find a home for her school, hire administrative and instructional staff, and kick-off a campaign to attract students to her school.

Hiring Staff and Creating Infrastructure.

Assuming that Mary's goal is to enroll one hundred students in her first year—fifty students in each of two grades, kindergarten and first, she is likely going to have to hire between eight and ten teachers, plus classroom aides. Mary has been appointed school director by her board, so the role of "principal" is filled, but Mary will also need administrative and secretarial staff, a facilities manager, and two security guards. As mentioned earlier, Mary has a lot of staff to hire with a small budget—especially during her start-up years, when her fixed costs are high in relation to her total budget. The reality might end up being that instead of hiring a facilities manager, Mary adds this hat to her growing collection of hats. Her first-year structure might look very different than her four-year structure, simply as a function of budget and prioritization.

Mary is also going to have to think carefully about whom she wants to hire as staff. She will also have to be careful about local politics. If she recruits teachers who are already teaching at district schools, she may come into conflict with union hiring rules when teachers who decide they want to teach at CARE Academy decide to resign from their positions. Because Mary's school is so small, she is unlikely to be faced with a statutory requirement that her teachers remain part of the collective bargaining agreement in effect in her district—but that is not to say that the local teachers union is going to make life easy for Mary and her school.

Marketing and PR: Attracting Parents . . . and Their Children.

How is the CARE Academy going to recruit its goal of one hundred students for its first year? Mary and her team are going to have to launch a public awareness and marketing campaign to let local parents know about her school—and to convince them that the CARE Academy charter school is a better option for their children than any other public school, or charter school, around. Her campaign is going to need to target parents with young children, since this is going to be a K–5 school but is starting with only the first two grade levels. Her campaign is going to have to define what kind of student this school will work best for, though in the end,

Mary's ability to control her student population will be somewhat limited, as she'll have to take any and all prospective students—customers—to fill her seats and make her budget. And, Mary is prohibited by federal law, and most state laws, from placing any admissions restrictions on her student body. In short, she must respect the same admissions policy as local public schools, which means being open to any student who wishes to attend, up to the point where she ceases to have room for more students.

If Mary is lucky enough to have more students want to attend her school than she has room for, she will need to establish a waiting list and a random admissions policy. Most states encourage (and most schools employ) a lottery system. Of course, there are some categories of students that may legally receive preferential treatment—students of school faculty members or siblings of children who already attend a charter school, for example. And, depending on the state, there are some provisions for maintaining a racial or ethnic balance in charter school populations as a way to use them as a tool to encourage public school integration.

Non-Educational Services: Buses, Lunch, Security, and Technology.
Mary is a teacher—and a budding entrepreneur. She knows well elementary education, professional development, and instructional design. She led a successful entrepreneurial effort to create a charter school. But there are some school functions for which she has little or no experience: how to provide lunch to more than one hundred students a day, how to coordinate transportation, how to hire and manage school security and develop a school security plan, how to purchase and administer payroll and benefits programs, and how to select the appropriate administrative and instructional technology. Mary is going to need help.

If she's lucky, she has room in her budget to hire someone to serve in the capacity of chief operating officer, with key responsibility for most non-instructional issues. If she doesn't have this luxury, Mary is going to have to decide whether to try to learn about all of these areas fast, and manage all arrangements herself, or whether to outsource these functions to outside companies.

Phase IV: Year One and Beyond:
Students—and Their Parents—Arrive

In charter schools, as in much of life, things rarely go exactly according to plan. To survive, Mary's school must be sensitive to the needs of her population and her community—and remain nimble enough to respond to changing circumstances, including the actions of the surrounding district.

Changing Horses Midstream: Facing the Unexpected.
Mary had hoped to attract equal numbers of urban and suburban children and for her student body to reflect racial, economic, and ethnic diversity. But when registration day rolled around, Mary found that this was not to be. Despite her best efforts to publicize her school to suburban parents, she failed to attract them in any significant numbers. The vast majority of the CARE Academy's students were children of color who lived within walking distance of the school and who otherwise would have been assigned to traditional public schools with weak educational programs and performance. Mary thought she was starting a school to appeal to the intellectual needs of parents and children—a progressive and nurturing educational outpost that would nurture childrens' creativity and curiosity. But what Mary and her team ended up creating was a viable public school alternative for local parents who were relieved not to have to send their children to neighborhood schools.

The disconnect between expectations and reality forced Mary and her instructional staff to make quick adjustments to the curriculum. Most entering students were performing at lower levels than their lessons were geared toward. This presented both short- and long-term problems, as teachers not only had to adjust the first week, but the entire year of lesson plans.

Student Evaluation and Accountability.
The team's grand plans for a student evaluation system based on comprehensive portfolios were also forced into redesign. Before

students could be judged based on creative and proficient academic output, teachers would first have to address core competency issues. Few students entered kindergarten with the preparation necessary to start learning to read; the vast majority of students entering first grade performed well below the fiftieth percentile on a baseline test that the school administered in early September. The year was going to have to be focused on remediation and the basics instead of inquiry-based learning and experimental pedagogy. And as the months passed, it dawned on Mary and her faculty that to serve the students to the best of their ability, their initial vision for their school was going to have to change.

The new challenge: how to keep their ideals of inquiry and experiential education while also focusing on the basics. At the end of the day, if CARE Academy students couldn't pass the state-mandated tests, the school would be out of business. The team's initial vision for the school did not include students who arrived at the school with educational deficits—and so the faculty did not think they'd have to spend much time teaching the basics of reading and the fundamental mechanics of mathematics. They didn't think that the vast majority of their students would have any trouble passing state tests. The new reality was daunting—not only because it meant developing new curricula and assessment methods essentially on the fly, but also because the faculty Mary hired to join the CARE Academy team did so because they wanted to get away from under-performing students and the constant test-prep and remediation this population requires. The change in student body was also the beginnings of a faculty retention nightmare for Mary and her board.

New Facilities Challenges.
CARE Academy was lucky—it had attracted a generous benefactor who was willing to give the school both a donation to cover the cost of leasing space for its first two years of operation and a sizeable grant toward a capital fund that would be used to design and build a brand-new home for the school. But between the time the promises were made and the middle of the school's first year, the

benefactor's business failed, and he was left in the awkward position of having to retract his promise. CARE Academy was fortunate that the donor had given the first year's lease payment in a lump sum. But CARE's administrators and board of directors now faced a greater problem. The capital fund was now millions of dollars short, dashing hopes for their own building; under current funding levels, the school would not be able to afford the rent for year two without an outside donation. So halfway through the year, the CARE Academy team was faced with a series of decisions that will affect their ability to operate in the years to come: how to increase revenues to afford leased space, space that would have to grow each year, since the school planned to eventually serve 600 students, up from the one hundred enrolled in year one.

There are a number of options for Mary to consider. She could look for another benefactor who is willing to underwrite the cost of rent—but this is a potentially time-consuming undertaking with no guarantee that the prospecting work will pay off. She could reconfigure her budget in search of ways to afford space under current PPE funding levels—but this would likely result in cutbacks in already bare-bones instructional budgets. Mary could consider increasing her projected enrollment—more students would mean more revenue, though it would also mean that the academy would need more space. Depending on the state where Mary's school is located, she might be able to apply to a state-administered facilities grant plan, to cover some of the costs associated with building or renovating space. In some states, charter schools are eligible to receive proceeds from state bond issues and direct these dollars toward capital projects. Regardless of which path she chooses, Mary is going to have to use her board of directors and work every angle she can to find a suitable solution.

Phase V: Accountability and Evaluation—Staying in Business

A few years into operation, Mary has established a thriving charter school and she and her team have learned how to keep their school open for business. She's mastered the art of fulfilling state requirements and paperwork; become savvy and skilled at obtaining state and federal categorical funds and private grants; and created an academic program that has gotten results—including yearly increases in the percentage of students who perform well on state-mandated math and English tests. Mary's school is well on its way to establishing itself as a permanent part of the local educational scene.

Dealing with Bureaucracy.

One of the reasons that Mary and her team of teachers and administrators were attracted to the charter concept was the prospect of being free from the red tape and, most of all, the onerous paperwork of the existing system. But like many promises of the charter school concept, this one was not quite to be. Though the CARE Academy is free from many rules and regulations that apply to traditional schools, it is not free from having to document and record many aspects of their school's operations. And because the school is an autonomous body, the CARE Academy's very existence relies on the timely and thorough submission of information to the chartering entity.

If the school fails to submit attendance information to the state on a regular basis, it simply will not receive any operating funds it does not have a district to fall back on or to run interference. If the school fails to submit applications for federal categorical aid, it will not receive the extra dollars necessary to meet the needs of the large low-income population. If all appropriate paperwork is not filed with the contracted bus company, the students won't even make it to school. When the time comes to administer standardized tests and use the results to determine student advancement, paperwork is what moves this process forward, and on and on. Whereas traditional public schools do have a lot of data to collect and paper to push, they also have the cushion of a district office, with specialized staff to deal with federal grant programs, transportation issues, and the like. Charter schools are often out on their own, with nobody but themselves to rely on. And with the limited administrative staff at many charter schools, the burden of administrative paperwork is heavy.

Selling Success.

With plans to add two grades per year for the next two years, CARE Academy must develop a long-term recruitment plan to ensure that the school has enough students to reach its goal capacity and continue to attract a steady stream of five-year-old kindergarten students to keep its enrollment pipeline full. This means Mary and her team must implement an effective, low-cost strategy for establishing a positive profile in their community and presenting themselves as an excellent educational choice.

What tools does she have at her disposal? Parents, who can help spread the word through word-of-mouth; community leaders, whom Mary was careful to cultivate during the charter application process, and whom she can now rely upon for support; the local print and television media, who have already profiled her school positively and whom she hopes will continue to do just that; and local business leaders, who have already embraced Mary as a common spirit—educational entreprenurism isn't all that different than business entrepreneurism—and who can make sure that the general business community knows about Mary and her school.

It's a lot of work, and without a full-time director of admissions, it's work that must be done by people without formal marketing or public relations experience. If CARE Academy is lucky, one of Mary's nonprofit or business partners will agree to dedicate staff time to helping the school articulate its message. If not, it's yet another non-instructional task that will fall to Mary, another problem that traditional public schools do not have to face.

Winning Renewal: The Cycle Begins Anew. . . .

Charter schools, by definition, must continually prove that they are working to stay in business. They may be subject to yearly performance reviews and financial audits and asked to prove that they are complying with all civil rights and Americans with Disabilities Act regulations. Whether the CARE Academy will continue to exist depends, theoretically, on the outcomes of these yearly reviews and of the culminating review that takes place near the end of the initial charter period.

As Mary's school evolves—like all charter schools, the CARE Academy is different in practice than it was on the paper of the original charter process—her accountability goals may change. Her pedagogy and curriculum may change. Her student achievement levels may go up or down, and some of that may be attributable to things almost entirely out of the school's control, like the socioeconomic status of the children who attend her school, and so on. Even with strict accountability guidelines for charter schools on the books, there are many situations and circumstances that might justify the charter's renewal even if performance goals haven't been met. Indeed, the vast majority of charter school closures to date are due to financial mismanagement or structural failure, rather than to student performance issues.

Which brings us back to a central question of the charter movement: If it is the case that the CARE Academy may, in fact, fail to meet its student performance goals, but stays open anyway because of mitigating factors, how, then, is this charter school different than the traditional school down the block? After five years, the duration of the initial charter, the CARE Academy community of parents, teachers, students, and community supporters are convinced that their school is doing things that would be impossible within the confines of the existing system. Parents are happy, students seem to be learning, and there is some demonstrated improvement by students on state reading and math tests, though the results are not substantially different than those reported by neighborhood schools. But with age and size comes the risk of complacency. Looking ahead to its next five years, CARE Academy will serve 600 students per year, employ nearly thirty teachers and eight administrators, and have a budget of close to $3.3 million per year. It's well on its way to becoming an institution, with its own entrenched bureaucracy. And though it has been a rewarding and fulfilling experience for all involved—including Mary, who realized her own personal dream of creating a school in her own image—the jury is still out as to whether the CARE Academy has contributed to school reform in its own community or within the American public school system at large.

THE MANY FACES OF CHARTER SCHOOLS: SIX STATES, SIX SCENARIOS

Because charter schools have evolved on a state-by-state basis, and each state's charter-enabling legislation is unique, there is no charter school state that can be considered truly representative of all others, or of the movement as a whole. Indeed, the charter movement is as diverse, and some would say, as strong, as it is decentralized. Though, as discussed above, all charter school laws share many key elements, the politics, implementation, and practice vary widely between and among the thirty-seven states and the District of Columbia that have passed charter-enabling legislation. To illustrate the many differences in how charter laws have been created and applied across the country, we have chosen six states with charter laws—Arizona, California, Michigan, Minnesota, Mississippi, and New York—which we will profile in the pages ahead.

New York

Year Law Passed: 1998
Number of Charters Approved, as of Spring 2001: 23
Length of Charter: Five years
Chartering Entities: New York City Board of Education, New York State Board of Regents, and the Board of Trustees of the State University of New York. Only the New York State Board of Regents is actually authorized to grant charters—charter applications approved by either of the other two chartering entities are forwarded to the Board of Regents, which then issues the official charter.

Other Charter Law Highlights:

- Charter schools must serve at least fifty students and employ at least three teachers;
- Charter schools must not impose admissions requirements;
- There can be an unlimited number of conversion charter schools, but a maximum of one hundred new charter schools;
- Teachers in most new charter schools are not required to participate in collective bargaining agreements, though collective bargaining agreements remain in effect for teachers at schools that convert to charter status;
- Preference is given to charter school applications that "demonstrate the capability to provide comprehensive learning experiences to students identified by the applicants as at risk of academic failure."

The New York Charter Schools Act of 1998 was passed late in the year—right before the state legislature's December recess. It was the result of a compromise between the pro-charter administration of Republican Governor George E. Pataki and the not-so-pro-charter forces, led by the United Federation of Teachers president, Randi Weingarten, and the speaker of the Democrat-controlled New York State Assembly, Sheldon Silver. The compromise allowed for collective bargaining agreements to remain in effect for all charter schools that are converted from existing public schools and for establishing collective bargaining units in any new charter school that serves more than 250 students. The establishment of three chartering entities alleviated fears that the chartering process would be tightly controlled by the governor, and some limits on the number of charter schools helped to allay fears that charter schools would drain funds from the existing public school system.

By fall 1999, less than six months after the first set of charters were approved, there were already a handful of schools in operation—a sign that many groups had been working hard, pre-legislatively, in anticipation of the time when they would be able to submit a charter application. Since 1998, the Charter Schools Institute at the State University of New York has established itself as a resource and advocate for charter schools. It also administers three important funding programs for New York State Charter Schools: the State Stimulus Fund Seed Grants (for individuals or organizations who are developing a charter school application), Start-Up Grants (for the holders of approved charters), and the Federal Public Charter Schools Program Planning and Implementation Grants (also for holders of approved charters).

As of fall 2001, New York State had approved thirty-nine charters and thirty of these schools were in operation (the remaining nine deferred their opening until, in most cases, fall 2002). Sixty-five percent of New York State charter schools are run by non-profit groups and 35 percent are run in partnership with for-profit EMOs, a ratio that is higher than in the rest of the country. New York City does not follow this pattern. Of twenty charter schools in operation there, all but four—75 percent—are run by nonprofit organizations. This overwhelming trend toward nonprofit, community-controlled charter schools in New York City is likely related to the controversial events of early 2001, when a proposal by Edison Schools, Inc., to take over the management of five troubled public schools—and to run them as conversion charter schools— was soundly defeated by parents at all five schools, despite the best efforts of Edison to win their approval.

New York City Schools Chancellor Harold O. Levy, in an attempt to radically revitalize these five schools—all of which had long been at the bottom of the New York State list of worst-performing schools—supported the idea of having Edison take over the management of these schools. Nothing else had worked at these schools, and to Levy, Edison was a pragmatic experiment in school reform. However, Levy selected these schools as potential Edison sites before consulting with the parents and community surrounding each school, and his plan was met with hostility and resistance. After a few months of attempting to drum up parental support for the conversion plan, including a half-million dollar public relations gift from the board of education to Edison, the conversion proposal failed to draw the required 50 percent of parental votes in any school.

Arizona

Year Law Passed: 1994
Number of Charters Approved, as of Spring 2001: 416
Length of Charter: Fifteen years
Chartering Entities: The Arizona Chartering Board and the Arizona State Board of Education may each approve up to twenty-five charters per year—but there is no limit on the number of charter schools that local school boards may charter each year.
Other Charter Law Highlights:

- Charter schools may be operated by for-profit organizations;
- Local school boards may authorize charter schools outside of their district;
- Charter schools receive state aid to support transportation of students to charter schools;
- Nonprofit charter schools may apply for facilities financing from state Industrial Development Authorities (IDA);
- Flexible collective bargaining rules for teachers—ranging from schools where teachers work independently to those where union work rules remain in effect.

Arizona, among the first states to embrace charters as a reform effort, is perhaps the state with the greatest variety of charter activity. Arizona is home to chains of for-profit charter schools and to charter schools that open and operate hundreds of miles from the district that sponsored their charter. The Arizona law encourages educational entrepreneurism; Arizona is a veritable petri dish for experiments in the educational market.[43] However, it is an experiment that is running without an equivalent control group against which to evaluate progress or define success or failure, as no other state comes close to the degree and diversity of Arizona's charter activity.

As of the 2000–2001 school year, Arizona had 403 charter schools in operation—which translates to nearly 20 percent of all charter schools *nationwide*. Statewide statistics are equally interesting. One in five Arizona public schools—22 percent—are charter schools, though they serve only 6 percent of Arizona students. Clearly, Arizona charter schools are smaller than traditional schools. It's not surprising that Arizona leads the nation in the number of charter schools that have ceased to operate. By the end of the 2000–2001 school year, more than forty-three Arizona charter schools had closed. Reasons for closures range from consolidation of sites to financial mismanagement to outright fraud.

Arizona has instituted a number of financial assistance plans designed to help charter schools meet their infrastructure-related costs. In addition to a $400-per-student grant that the state provides to charter schools to cover capital and operational costs, funding above and beyond the per-pupil allocation, Arizona has also established a state Stimulus Fund, administered by the State Department of Education. This fund provides grants of up to $100,000 to first-year charter schools to cover start-up or facilities-related costs, with schools eligible for up to an additional $100,000 in grants for related infrastructure needs.

In addition, Arizona authorizes charter schools that are run by nonprofit organizations to obtain financing from Industrial Development Authorities—local entities that can issue debt in the form of bonds and lend the proceeds to qualified groups, including charter schools. As reported by the Center for Educational Reform in a 2000 Action Paper, one Arizona IDA—the Maricopa County IDA—used the pooled proceeds from a $27 million bond sale to finance the capital needs of seven Arizona charter schools. The Maricopa IDA received an investment-grade debt rating on its bonds, setting an interesting precedent around the use of investment debt to finance public charter schools.[44]

With Arizona's permissive charter law—particularly the provision that charter schools do not have to operate within the boundaries of the district that authorizes their charter—there have been a number of cases of schools and districts where financial entrepreneurism has reached new heights. One striking example of this is the Window Rock school district in Arizona. A small district, with a limited number of schools and limited revenue, Window Rock realized that the Arizona charter law would allow the administration to approve large numbers of charters, each of which would result in administrative fees for the district while costing next to nothing in terms of ongoing expenditures. Window Rock put the word out that it was open for the business of approving charters—and soon, allegations spread that in fact, Window Rock was actually selling charters in exchange for large yearly administrative fees from charter operators. Once exposed, Window Rock withdrew from the chartering business altogether, leaving schools with Window Rock charters looking for new sponsors.[45]

California

Year Law Passed: 1992
Number of Charters Approved, as of Spring 2001: 302
Length of Charter: Five years
Chartering Entities: Local school boards.
Other Charter Law Highlights:

- Home-based charter schools are acceptable under state law;
- Charter districts—where all schools in a given district are converted to charter status—may be created if at least 50 percent of teachers in a given district sign a petition and with the approval of the California State Board of Education and the superintendent of public instruction;
- California's charter law specifically seeks to support the creation of charters that "increase learning opportunities for all students, with special emphasis on expanded learning opportunities for pupils who are identified as academically low-achieving."[46] ;
- Though existing public schools may convert from traditional to charter status, private schools may not.

Since California, the second state to pass charter legislation, has long been the site of legislative battles over public education— from funding to bilingual education—it is not surprising that California charter schools are both wildly popular and wildly controversial. California's charter schools run the gamut from Internet-based individual instruction programs serving students who are essentially home-schooled to large urban high schools that have turned their educational programs around and drastically improved student performance since converting to charter status. Nearly 40 percent of California's charter schools were traditional public schools before electing to convert to charter status—perhaps a sign of community support for individual schools but disdain for educational bureaucracy. California's charter law even makes it possible for entire public school districts to convert to charter status; to date, three districts have followed this path.

The rise of California's charter movement is attributable to efforts by Democratic legislators to hold back the voucher movement in the early 1990s. As written by a Democratic state senator, Gary K. Hart, the charter law sought to provide families with greater choice among schools without "threatening public schools."[47] In the senator's words, "It seemed possible to us to craft a legislative proposal that did not sacrifice the attractive features of the voucher movement—namely, choice of schools, local control, and responsiveness to clients—while still preserving the basic principles of public education: that it be free, non-sectarian, and nondiscriminatory." California's original charter law was moderately strong, though it contained a cap on the number of charter schools that could be approved and provisions that at least 10 percent of teachers within the district where a school was going to be newly created, or half of the teachers in a conversion school, approve of the charter effort. In 1998, California's law was amended and the climate for charter schools became much friendlier. The cap on the number of schools was raised from one hundred to 250, with provision for an additional one hundred schools per year, and it became easier to obtain a charter.[48] Today, California is home to a thriving charter school community, with 358 schools up and running for the 2001–2002 school year.

Michigan

Year Law Passed: 1993
Number of Charters Approved, as of Spring 2001: 185

Length of Charter: Up to ten years, with a mandatory review at least every seven years—but most charters awarded to date have been for five years, with renewal pending review at the end of the initial award period.

Chartering Entities: Local school boards, intermediate school boards, community colleges, and state public universities.

Other Charter Law Highlights:

- No limit on the number of charters that may be authorized; only restriction is that no single university may authorize more than 50 percent of charters issued by all universities combined;
- Existing private schools may convert to charter school status;
- If a charter petition submitted to a local school board is rejected, the applicant may have it placed on the local ballot for popular vote;
- Teachers in schools authorized by local school boards are covered by district collective bargaining agreements—but teachers in charter schools authorized by other entities are not.

Michigan is one of the nation's most active charter school states, with an expansive law that state charter school proponents say *still* isn't strong enough. Nearly 4 percent of Michigan students attend one of the state's 200 charter schools, nearly 20 percent of which are located in Detroit, one of the state's poorest troubled cities. One of the more interesting aspects of Michigan's charter school law is that it includes a provision that allows rejected charter applicants to appeal the decision by having their application placed on a local ballot, with the public deciding the merit of their school plan.

As of October 2001, nearly 200 charter schools, or Public School Academies (PSAs) as they are called in Michigan, were open for business. The vast majority (nearly three-quarters) of these schools are authorized by universities—a much larger percentage than in any other charter state. One reason for this phenomenon may be that charter schools that are authorized by universities have much more flexibility in hiring faculty. University-authorized charter schools are able to employ experienced community college instructors or university tenure-track faculty, regardless of whether they

are state-certified teachers, while charter schools authorized by local school boards must comply with the same teacher certification
requirements as traditional Michigan public schools. A second reason may be that there is a small, though not insignificant, financial
incentive for post-secondary institutions that serve as chartering
agencies; under state law, they receive 3 percent of the state operating aid for each school they charter.

Though support for charter schools in Michigan is widespread,
so is resistance. The Center for Educational Reform reported in
2001 that the question of whether to amend the state's charter law
to eliminate a cap on the number of charter schools remains unre-
solved. Governor John Engler, a Republican, is a strong supporter
of the move to eliminate the charter school cap.[49] A blue-ribbon
panel, led by Peter McPherson, president of Michigan State University, was appointed to review the issue and make recommendations. In Michigan, state universities are included on the list of
state-authorized chartering entities. However, from the Center of
Education Reform's perspective, this panel is biased against the
removal of a cap, as the center pointed out in its *Newswire* e-
newsletter on October 10, 2001: "Although 150 charters have been
authorized by (Michigan) universities, none have been chartered
by the institution McPherson heads, raising questions about any
predisposition he might hold."

Another Michigan charter school controversy surrounds the
decision of Bay Mills Community College, a small, Native Ameri-
can-run college in the Upper Peninsula, to authorize two charter
schools hundreds of miles away from the college's Brimley,
Michigan, location. These schools, which opened in Bay City and
Pontiac in 2001, are to be run by New York City-based Mosaica
Education. What makes this situation even more interesting is
that Michigan's charter legislation seems to indicate that there
would be no limit on the number of charter schools that Bay
Mills could ultimately authorize, unlike the limits on all other
state chartering agencies. Because Bay Mills is run by a Native
American tribal council that is charged with serving Native
American students statewide and operates without fixed district

boundaries, tribal leadership maintains that they have the authority to authorize charter schools throughout the state.[50] In the end, one question raised by the Bay Mills controversy is this: Can Bay Mills effectively sponsor an end-run around the legislative deadlock over a cap on the number of Michigan charter schools?

Minnesota

Year Law Passed: 1991
Number of Charters Approved, as of Spring 2001: 68
Length of Charter: Initial charter is granted for up to three years
Chartering Entities: Local school boards; public post-secondary institutions; private colleges; and cooperatives. All charters must be approved by the state Board of Education, which has the power to grant charters on appeal.
Other Charter Law Highlights:

- The Minnesota charter law allows for an unlimited number of charter schools;
- A local school board may authorize a charter for a school to be operated outside of the authorizing district's boundaries if the district where the school will operate agrees;
- Existing private schools may convert to charter status;
- Though all Minnesota students are theoretically entitled to attend any school within the state of their choosing, and though enrollment requirements are not permitted for any charter school, if a charter school limits enrollment to residents of a high-concentration minority area, the school's student body must reflect racial balance of the area; hence preference may be given to certain students to ensure compliance with this requirement.

As the first state to pass charter legislation—and the home of the nation's first charter school—Minnesota can rightly be considered the birthplace, and the incubator, of the charter school movement. Over the years, Minnesota's charter law has served as an inspiration for many other states' charter legislation, and its local charter school heroes—Ted Kolderie and Joe Nathan—have tirelessly traveled the country preaching the gospel of charter schools. Their respective home institutions—the Center for Policy Studies and the Center for School Change at the University of Minnesota's Humphrey Institute for Public Affairs—actively promote charter schools as the education reform policy most likely to drive real improvement in our nation's public schools. And in 2000, nearly ten years after Minnesota's law was passed by the state legislature, the Minnesota Charter School Law—and the legislature that passed it—received the Innovations in American Government Award from Harvard University's Institute for Government Innovation—which also meant an award of $100,000 from the Ford Foundation to benefit Minnesota charter schools.

What does the charter landscape look like in the movement's home state? For starters, charters are not as common as one might think. Only about 1 percent of the state's public school students are enrolled in charter schools. Nearly half of all charter schools are concentrated in Minneapolis and St. Paul. According to a 1999 study, far fewer charter school students met Minnesota state graduation requirements in both English and math than did a comparable group of public school students. It is also true—which may account for the low performance of charter school students—that nearly half of all Minnesota charter school students are classified as economically disadvantaged (as opposed to 24 percent of all Minnesota students), nearly half were new to their school in the year examined by the study, and nearly half live in Minneapolis-St. Paul.[51] Lastly, the state's law has continued to be amended—most recently, to lift the cap on the number of charter schools that may be created and to add universities to the list of chartering entities.

There are many options for starting a charter school in Minnesota. Prospective charter operators can choose between local school boards, public post-secondary institutions, private colleges, and cooperatives (though all applications are subject to state Board of Education approval). In 1999, the Minnesota legislature approved a plan that would provide new charter schools with grants of up to $50,000 (or $500 times the number of students served, whichever is greater) during the first two years of operation. Minnesota also provides for "lease aid" to charter schools, to help schools that choose to lease a building or land for their schools. Schools apply to the state to receive this aid, which is provided to schools that do not have sufficient operating capital to cover the cost of lease payments.

Mississippi

Year Law Passed: 1997
Number of Charters Approved, as of Spring 2001: 1
Length of Charter: Initial charter is granted for four years
Chartering Entities: State Board of Education, following local board approval of petition.
Other Charter Law Highlights:

- State law authorizes a maximum of six charter schools statewide;
- Only existing public schools may apply to convert to charter status; new charter schools are not permitted;
- Mississippi charter schools may not be managed or operated by for-profit organizations;
- Charter school teachers remain district employees.

Though Mississippi does, technically, have a charter school law on its books, it would be a stretch to call Mississippi a charter school state. The current law authorizes a maximum of six charter schools statewide—one in the Mississippi Delta region and one in each of the state's five congressional districts. Only conversion schools are permitted, and teachers in charter schools remain employees of the local district. According to the Center for Education Reform, Mississippi's charter law has the distinction of being "the weakest of the nation's thirty-eight charter laws."[52] Perhaps even more indicative of Mississippi's attitude toward charter schools is the fact that a 2002 search of the Mississippi

Department of Education's Web site turned up no mention of the state's charter law, charter initiative, or even of its single charter school—the Hayes Cooper Center in Merigold, located in Mississippi's Delta region.

The Hayes Cooper Center for Math, Science and Technology, which proudly bills itself on its Web site as "the first and only charter school in Mississippi," serves more than 300 students in grades kindergarten to sixth. It opened as a charter school in the fall of 1998 after converting from a "regular" public school. According to Richard Roberson, the charter school contact at the Mississippi Department of Education, Hayes Cooper was already a "pretty good" school before it converted to charter status, and it did so to have the freedom to try new and innovative instructional strategies. The current principal, Beverly Hardy, was the principal before conversion, and under her leadership, the school has continued to thrive. Last year, the school's fifth grade students led the state in performance on state-administered standardized tests. The school integrates computers and technology into the curriculum starting in pre-K and also has innovative programs in science and math.

Because of the restrictive nature of Mississippi's law, charter activity has been extremely limited. As of 2002, there were no charter applications under review. According to Roberson, anecdotal evidence shows that the vast majority of inquiries about charter schools received by the state Department of Education are from groups of disgruntled parents or community members who are in disagreement with school leadership or local school boards—and who see charter conversion as a way to take control of their school. However, these inquiries rarely, if ever, result in a serious charter application. The state does hear from groups or individuals who want to start charter schools, but because the law does not currently provide for this option, they are turned away.

The tide may be turning for Mississippi's charter law, however. When the law was passed in 1997, the movement was not yet as strong as it is now, and the law's weakness may have resulted from a general lack of information on the part of state legislators. During the 2001 legislative session, the state approved a measure that extended Mississippi's charter law until 2004. More recently, there has been some movement to increase the number of chartering agencies and to change the law so that charters could be awarded to new schools—and, according to Roberson, it seems fairly certain that the Mississippi state legislature will revisit charters during the 2002 legislative session.

PROJECTIONS VERSUS ACTUALS: HAVE CHARTER SCHOOLS FULFILLED THE PROMISE?

For well over a decade, some of the country's leading authorities on educational reform have argued strongly that competition is the key to school improvement. This argument is based on an economic theory dear to the heart of theoretical capitalism—supply and demand. We say theoretical because, in the real world of supply and demand, there are many intervening variables: advertising, fashion, fear, and government intervention. In a society as saturated by advertising as ours, it is difficult to distinguish between need, imaginary need, real demand, and created demand. This is particularly true in the field of education.

What is the demand for education? This is a question that is seldom asked. There is a demand for credentials, but even that seemingly real demand is suffused with many subjective considerations, not the least of which is that educational credentials are strongly associated with social status. Not only does it matter how much schooling an individual has, but it also matters where he or she went to school. Almost none of the literature concerning educational reform comes to grips with the fact that where one goes to school is more important in many cases than what one learned in school. As a consequence, competition never really occurs on a level playing field. Privileged families bring to the playing field many social assets that are not available to less privileged families. The supply of schools that are available will always be linked to the larger society and the status hierarchy that structures social relations.

Charter schools are one experiment in introducing market forces to public education. While the charter school movement is not an expression of pure competition or free market values, it is a significant step in the direction of deregulation. One might think of charter schools as a government-sponsored experiment in privatizing a public institution. The early proponents of charter schools made sweeping claims for them: Charter schools would be more innovative than public schools. Charter school students would learn more and score higher on standardized tests than regular public school students. Charter school teachers and parents would be more deeply involved in education than the teachers and parents of children enrolled in regular public schools. And most importantly, charter schools would serve as examples of educational innovation that would encourage public school educators to raise their standards, become more imaginative, and generally revitalize public education.

Most early charter school advocates did not qualify their claims and certainly seemed unaware of the consistent research that school performance is only marginally related to its form of governance.[53] That is, school effectiveness is associated with the leadership qualities of principals, the creativity of teachers, and the academic climate of schools. There is also a very large and substantial body of research that confirms what most parents already know— the social class background of the children has a lot to do with the effectiveness of the school. There are many counter examples to this last finding but, in general, in the hierarchy of effective schools, one must be candid in admitting that the higher the social class background of the students, the more positive the academic climate of the school.

The charter school revolution claimed that it could lessen this relationship between privilege and achievement by creating schools that are smaller, more innovative and more motivational, and hold themselves to higher standards. The small-school movement appeared to provide the evidence that the key to equality of opportunity for all children is to create smaller schools, smaller classes, and more highly motivated teachers.

Charter schools have been in existence for ten years. A decade is a substantial amount of time and, therefore, it is fair to ask whether or not the charter school movement as a whole has fulfilled its promise. Of course, generalizations camouflage exceptions. It is a disservice to charter schools to single out a few failures and to use these failures as an example of the whole. Equally true, however, it is a disservice to the public to fasten on a few successful charter schools and then to argue they represent all charter schools. To assess whether or not charter schools have fulfilled their promise, we are dependent upon a wide variety of researchers. Some of these researchers are frank advocates and some are frank opponents. Almost all research should be taken with a grain of salt. Because the school choice movement is so deeply politicized and touches on fundamental social sensitivities and political issues, we are best served by following a simple principle— all evidence should be treated as suggestive and the conclusions that are drawn should be treated as tentative.

This kind of caution does not satisfy those that who are seeking a thumbs up or a thumbs down about charter schools. But it is an intellectually prudent position because, as we'll see, the research is mixed. Where some researchers see charter schools as highly innovative, others see them as quite predictable. Where some researchers believe that there is strong evidence that charter school students out-perform similar students from regular public schools, others see mixed results at best.

In this section we examine the research concerning the observable results of the charter school movement. As the reader will see, our overall evaluation of this reform is closer to a B than it is to an A or an F. Moreover, there are areas in which charter schools appear to have succeeded and there are areas where they have not had the impact that their advocates have claimed for them. We will examine the research concerning charter schools in the following areas: student achievement, curricular innovation, student-to-teacher ratio, accountability, access, and impact.

Student Achievement

One of the early fears of the opponents of charter schools was that they would not be held accountable in the same way as regular public schools. In states with strong chartering laws, charter schools are held to a high level of accountability. Moreover, it is evident that the founders of charter schools are evaluating themselves, at least in part according to standardized tests. According to the Center for Education Reform, 97 percent of charter schools reported administering at least one standardized test. Seventy-three percent require a state-specific test and 42 percent require the Stanford Nine.

Thus far, there is very little systematic data across states that would allow us to evaluate the overall academic success of charter schools. Chester Finn, Bruno Manno, and Greg Vanourek acknowledge the lack of systematic data, but cite the research of the Center for School Change at the University of Minnesota, which claims that two-thirds of the charter schools show significant achievement gains.[56] This claim is buttressed by other small-scale studies such as one in Colorado, which found that charter school students outperformed regular public school students.[57] According to the Center for Education Reform, there is considerable individual school and anecdotal data that shows charter school students outperform comparable regular public school students.[58]

The story of charter schools and student achievement is, however, quite complex. A 1999 Minnesota study found that 40 percent of charter pupils met the state's graduation requirement for math (compared with 71 percent of students statewide). And that 43 percent of charter pupils met the state's standards for reading (compared with 68 percent statewide).[59] Evidence from Arizona is also less than spectacular; according to the Goldwater Institute, thirty-five charter sites made gains in reading, math and language, while twenty declined in those subjects. This pattern of mixed results was also found in Texas, California, and Michigan.[60]

In fact, in Texas these lack of achievement results led a panel of state lawmakers to recommend a moratorium on new charter schools. Only 59 percent of charter school students passed a Texas state skills exam in the 1998–1999 school year, compared to the state average of 78.4 percent. In the summer of 2000, the Texas State Education Agency gave an "unacceptable" rating to nearly one-fourth of the 103 charter schools it studied. This kind of critical review was echoed in a National School Boards Association report that concluded, "There is very little evidence—across the board—to suggest that charters have been successful in raising student achievement, providing greater classroom innovation, strengthening accountability, or influencing traditional public schools."[61] In a study that analyzed five years of state testing data from 171 charter schools, researchers from Western Michigan University's Evaluation Center found that students at charter schools trailed their regular public school peers in absolute passing rates in all four subjects covered by the exams: reading, writing, mathematics, and science. Charter schools also generally showed less improvement in test scores over time when compared with students in their host districts. According to Gary Miron, a co-author of the study, "Charter schools have diverse missions, but student achievement has to be part of that."[62]

In fairness to charter schools, it should be noted that raising student achievement among students whose prior educational backgrounds are weak is a difficult task—a far more difficult task than the armchair educational reform warriors in universities, think tanks, and political offices would have us believe. Charter schools have not produced student achievement miracles. There are some charter schools that have done exceptionally well, as the data from the Center from Educational Reform indicates, but from a systemic point of view there is little to lead us to believe that charter schools are likely to become, as a group, beacons of hope for those who believe that deregulation and competition inevitably lead to higher student achievement.

Curricular Innovation

Proponents of charter schools might well argue that our current fetish with test scores is not an entirely useful measure when evaluating the worth of the charter school experiment. What matters is that charter schools are educational experiments where new ideas can be tested and creativity can be given the opportunity to flower. Earlier, we described in some depth the variety of missions that characterize charter schools. Charter schools are singular; by definition, charter schools are meant to break the mold. It may also be that the most important innovation of all is to take a traditional curriculum and do it very well; from the point of view of families, the most significant innovation might well be providing a safe, disciplined, and academically positive environment for their children.

However, the claims of charter school proponents have led us to believe that charter schools will be truly innovative and break new ground as we struggle for educational models for the twenty-first century. According to the U.S. Department of Education, nearly two-thirds of newly created charter schools seek to realize an alternative vision of schooling, and an additional one-quarter of newly created schools were founded primarily to serve a special target population of students. While the founders of charter schools may have an alternative vision of education, there is very little systematic evidence that charter schools are in any way educationally revolutionary in terms of curriculum and instruction. In a 1998 study, headed by Amy Stuart Wells, it was found that, generally speaking, charter schools were not serving as laboratories for public schools. In response, the Center for Educational Reform reported that in the academic year 2000–2001, 29 percent of charter schools had a science, math, and technology focus, 23 percent focused on basic skills, 20 percent considered themselves to be college prep, and 22 percent characterized themselves as emphasizing direct instruction.[63] None of these categories could be considered educationally revolutionary.

Perhaps the reason charter schools, as a group, have not demonstrated the boldness of vision that their advocates hoped for them can be explained by the following: (1) Most parents have traditional ideas about education and are not that interested in educational experimentation; (2) The number of teachers and principals who are truly innovative may be far fewer than we imagined; and (3) The importance of standardized testing requires all schools to emphasize those subjects and topics that are tested.

The issue of innovation, however, needs further exploration because charter school advocates in their effort to denigrate public education may have put themselves so far out on an ideological limb that they can easily be sawed off, not by their opponents, but by their own hands. Many regular public schools are quite innovative and have far more resources for innovation than do charter schools. Individual educational pioneers generally will have a difficult time competing with larger well-financed educational institutions. As a consequence, a charter school's capacity to create and institutionalize innovative practices may be quite limited. If the demand for schooling is traditional, then the supply of schools will also be traditional.

Student-to-Teacher Ratio

Research continually demonstrates that class size is a critical variable in promoting student achievement. In smaller classes, students are more likely to receive individual attention. Teachers are more likely to take a genuine interest in their students. There is less time wasted due to discipline problems, and smaller classes can produce the camaraderie that is the heart and soul of an energized focused classroom. We have already seen that charter schools are small compared to regular public schools. But is their student-to-teacher ratio higher or lower than regular public schools?

In January 2000, the U.S. Department of Education reported that charter schools had a slightly lower student-to-teacher ratio than did all public schools in the states studied.[64] The median student-to-teacher ratio for charter schools was 16.0 as compared to 17.2 for all public schools. The most noticeable difference between the charter school and regular public school median student-to-teacher ratios was at the ungraded schools, with ungraded charter schools having a much higher student-to-teacher ratio, 18.8 students per teacher as compared to 8.8 students per teacher in other public schools. Class sizes in elementary charter schools are likely to be smaller when compared to other public elementary schools. Charter schools that served high school students tended to have class sizes that were the same or larger than at other public schools.

For charter school advocates, this is not good news. When we take away the rhetoric and examine the reality, it turns out that charter schools are not significantly different than other public schools on a key indicator. Charter school advocates make a great to-do about how charter schools have long waiting lists for students who wish to attend them. According to the Center for Education Reform, the average waiting list for a charter school is 112 students or 43 percent of the average charter school's enrollment.[65] But what are the parents waiting for? If the student-to-teacher ratio is the same as in other public schools, they may be waiting for an educational opportunity for their children that may only be a promise, not a reality.

Accountability

In June 2001 the U.S. Department of Education, through the Office of Educational Research and Improvement, issued the *National Charter School Accountability Study*, the lead author of which is Paul Hill of the University of Washington.[66] This very thorough study covers a wide variety of topics related to accountability. The researchers studied how charter schools develop internal accountability, how they manage accountability relationships with parents and teachers, how they manage accountability with voluntary agencies, and how charter school accountability can be improved.

Essentially, the authors view accountability in terms of the web of relationships that enfold charter schools. The authors' major findings were: "Though charter schools experience periods of confusion as they are starting up, most quickly learn that the best way to maintain the confidence of authorizers, families, teachers and donors is to focus on providing quality instruction." The authors go on to list several other issues that they uncovered in their research, which include maintaining communication with multiple constituents, setting up governing boards that work, establishing accountability procedures that emphasize performance rather than compliance, and coping with the fact that some government agencies are tougher on charter schools than they are on conventional public schools.

The authors of this study emphasize that most charter school operators are learning by doing and make several key recommendations, which include improving relationships with governing boards, seizing the initiative in terms of external accountability, becoming wise consumers, and, for the authorizers, taking responsibilities toward charters seriously. The authors conclude, "Charter schooling is the laboratory in which governments and other actors, both public and private, can learn how to play new roles in public school accountability. Charter schools, once a marginal enterprise, can offer new insights to renewal in public education."[67]

Amy Stuart Wells and her colleagues in their study of seventeen California charter schools found that in California charter schools were not being held accountable for enhanced academic achievement of their students; they were more likely to be held fiscally accountable.[68] School boards were ambivalent about their responsibilities to monitor charter schools. These researchers also found that the amount of public funding received for operating expenses ranged widely from one district to the next and even within the same district. These investigators also found that private sources are necessary for the survival of charter schools and that charter schools often depend on strong well-connected leaders for survival.

One positive that does emerge from these studies is that many charter schools have established strong relationships with the families they serve. In their 2000 study, Chester E. Finn Jr. and his colleagues spent considerable time emphasizing the satisfaction level of students and parents.[69] Of course, since the students and parents had made their choice of a school, one would expect there to be a positive response to questions concerning levels of satisfaction. Relying on a Hudson Institute 1997 survey of nearly 5,000 charter pupils, Finn and his colleagues report that what students like about charter schools are the teachers, the academic environment, the availability of technology, and the general atmosphere. What they do not like about charter schools are the poor sports programs, the lack of extracurricular activities, the food, and the insufficient technology.

The parents who send their children to charter schools, on average, are satisfied because of class size, school size, and the attention their children receive from the teachers. In a study conducted by Peter W. Cookson Jr., Catherine Embree, and Scott Fahey of six Edison schools in Michigan, Colorado, and California, five of which were charters, it was evident that parents who had chosen an Edison school for their children were satisfied with their choice and supported their school by donating considerable time and effort.[70] Parental satisfaction is not the same as parental oversight. Yet, there is no evidence that consumers are voting with their feet, as market proponents predict. Charter school advocates claim that competition will lead uncompetitive and poor schools to close. To date, however, charter school closures have been on account of low enrollment, or financial mismanagement, or embezzlement. Few have been closed because they are not living up to their academic charters or because families have forced charter school operators to change their educational approaches.

Accountability is a key word in the charter school lexicon of school virtues. Interestingly, the research indicates that forging accountability measures and evaluating schools according to those measures is a work in progress. Schools can be closed for financial problems because books can be audited. It is more difficult to close a school for academic problems because learning is difficult to measure—even by standardized tests. One conclusion that emerges from the research is that establishing marketplace discipline as a way of separating the winners from the losers has yet to create a convincing case that markets succeed when bureaucratic methods fail.

Access

One accusation that has been laid at the door of charter schools is that they skim the best students and leave the weakest students in the regular school system. There are those who claim that charter schools will re-stratify public schools by selecting the easiest to educate. In general, however, there is little evidence that charter schools are re-stratifying public education. A study by the Institute for Education and Social Policy at New York University found, "A closer analysis suggests that charter schools may be proliferating at both the low and high end of the race/ethnicity and affluence/poverty continuum. Whether this tendency will exacerbate racial isolation or create more isolation by social class among students remains to be seen."[71] In a paper in 2000, Carol Ascher and Nathalis Wamba of New York University's Institute for Education and Social Policy concluded with this disturbing finding, "Charter schools serving low income children of color are less likely to provide an academic curriculum, and are generally not as rich in educational resources, as charter schools serving white middle class students."[72]

The Impact of Charter Schools on Public Education

Charter school advocates argue that one of the major benefits of charter schools is that they will drive public education in the direction of innovation and accountability.[73] The charter school movement is not about creating a relatively small number of schools for a relatively small number of children, but it is a lever to break apart the bureaucratic stranglehold that traditional public education has over teachers and families. The assignment to reform public school education is a big one indeed.[74] It should be noted in fairness that education successes are seldom replicated. Schools tend to be their own little kingdoms and seldom borrow from others. The diffusion of innovation is complex, long-term and uncertain. From what we know about innovation and education, there is very little reason to expect that single experiments will change other schools.

The issue of diffusion is critical if the competitive model of educational reform is to hold water. Americans have been forming private schools for over 300 years. Despite much of the rhetoric of the school choice movement, we know that there is a diversity of school options, at least for those that can afford them. Eleven percent of American children attend private school and virtually anybody is free to start a school if he or she can secure the financial support. Given this picture, what can we say about the ability of charter schools to revitalize other public schools or public school districts? James K. Glassman makes the argument that in Arizona, charter schools are pushing conventional public schools to innovate.[75] He refers to the fact that the Mesa Unified School District runs advertisements in the local papers to encourage students to attend Mesa Public Schools. Because the Mesa Public School System is losing millions of dollars in funds to charter schools, Mesa administrators have become more entrepreneurial and innovative.

In the California study of charter schools, however, Amy Stuart Wells and her associates found that there was little connection between charter schools and other schools. There was no mechanism in place for charter schools and conventional public schools to share their successes and failures and, thus, the pattern of continued isolation remained. There are even examples of charter schools that have uncharted themselves, such as International High School in New York City, because the school's leaders found that being a charter required even more paperwork and politics than a conventional school.

In a major study conducted by the U.S. Department of Education's Office of Research and Improvement, it was found that nearly half of the school district leaders in the study perceived that charter schools had negatively affected their budget and had reduced revenue for the operations of the non-charter schools. This study, entitled *Challenge and Opportunity: The Impact of Charter Schools on School Districts*, also found that nearly half of school district leaders reported becoming more customer-service oriented, increasing their marketing and public relations efforts, or increasing the frequency of interaction with parents. The study also found that most districts implemented new educational programs or created new schools with programs that were similar to the programs of the local charter schools.[76]

If these findings were correct, it would appear that charter schools could affect local conditions. By withdrawing funds from public school budgets to support charter schools, pressure can be put on local school districts to perform more effectively and, on a more positive note, charter schools can provide educational models for other schools.

This evidence suggests that in time charter schools may have some positive impact on public education, although there is no evidence that this impact is systematic or has resulted in upgrading the level of education for all students across all schools. Moreover, given the evidence that we have found thus far, the diffusion of innovation is not always to be encouraged if the innovation does not produce measurable results.

CONCLUSION

Thus far, we have examined the political and educational development of the charter school movement and have presented information about the challenges and promises inherent in creating a charter school. We have also attempted to communicate some of the idiosyncrasies of the national charter school movement, which as we have shown is actually an amalgamation of thirty-eight efforts—resulting in a decentralized and fragmented reform effort.

What we conclude is this:

- Creating a charter school, whether a conversion school or a new school, is extremely difficult. Charter schools receive markedly fewer resources, financial and otherwise, and charter school leaders are responsible for providing a much broader range of services to students than are leaders at traditional schools, as these schools have a district to look after them.
- While most charter schools emerge from a consistent set of motivations—the desire to be free from bureaucracy, free to

innovate without oversight, free to create unique educational environments—the charter school movement itself is quite fragmented.

- Once a charter school is established, it is often highly dependent on the efforts and charisma of the founding individual or team, which we believe poses the question, and the challenge, of what will happen to charter schools as their original leadership and faculty move on, as they eventually will.

- One of the promises of the charter movement was that as charter schools grew and succeeded, they would document and share their best practices with all schools, including neighboring traditional public schools. By doing so, charter schools would be helping to improve the entire system of public education. However, it seems that more often than not, this promise is broken. Running a charter school—or teaching at one, for that matter—is an incredibly time-consuming endeavor. There is usually no systematic easy way to share experiences, successes, and failures.

- To date, charter schools, as a group, have not demonstrated a measurable impact on student learning and have not yet produced systematic improvement in the public school system as a whole. In fact, in some cases charter school performance lags behind "regular" public school performance in terms of student achievement, curricular innovation, student-to-teacher ratio, accountability, and access. Charter schools are no silver bullets.[77]

- Our assessment is that the charter movement is quite fragile—and is not likely to directly result in the kind of watershed change in the American public education system as its founders predicted and its champions assert. Despite the best intentions of the movement's national leadership and of the vocal group of charter school founders and directors that form the core of the movement, we believe that the charter school movement will in the end have a limited impact on the system as a whole.

Though we do not advocate for the protection of the current educational bureaucracy, we believe strongly that many, if not most, American public school districts and schools could use a radical overhaul in administrative as well as in instructional design and process. We also believe that bureaucracies provide continuity and protection in times of transition. A public school that is linked to a larger community—of district schools, for example—has a built-in network within which to share student work, disseminate excellent curricula, and learn from each other's successes and failures. Charter schools are, for the most part, cut off from official, local school networks. Though it is true that many charter school founders, faculty, and leadership take advantage of the many Internet-based charter school resource centers and support groups, it is also true that there is nothing like face-to-face collaboration to spur on innovation and change.

If we are correct, and if the charter movement continues as a decentralized movement that supports the creation of locally designed and locally accountable public schools, we believe that in the near future, the charter movement may reach a plateau where its schools are not all that different than traditional public schools that have tried new initiatives and directions.

PART TWO:
The Social and Political
Geology of Charter Schools

Public education has always been contested ground; there was never a time when public education was not a political issue. From the beginning of the common school movement in Massachusetts in the 1830s to today, Americans have been arguing with each other about the purpose and effectiveness of public education. Left, right, and center regularly exchange places in an educational game of musical chairs. In the 1960s, radical critics of public education advocated for vouchers; in the early twenty-first century it is the conservatives who favor vouchers. Even the labels left, right, and center are unclear—a citizen can be "left" on the environment and "right" on abortion without suffering cognitive dissidence. This is because we have shifted from group loyalties to individual lifestyle loyalties and in doing so, transformed politics.

Yet, it is clear that since Ronald Reagan's presidency there has been a fairly unified movement from the right of the political spectrum, and this movement has successfully gained the commanding heights in shaping the national, political, and economic agenda. By "conservative," we mean someone who supports smaller government, believes in market solutions to public and economic challenges, and is usually pro-life, anti-gun control, and somewhat nostalgic for a past when social relations were less contentious.

Conservatives share certain values, but they are not a monolithic group. Nor do they agree with each other on every issue. In fact, the true radical right is far more libertarian than the "country club Republican." Be that as it may, conservatism is a worldview—a stance about public and private life and an ideological platform upon which political movements are created.

In the first part of this book, we examined charter schools and in this part we examine the politics of hope and despair. In particular, we ask ourselves why the charter school movement—and the school choice movement—has such a wide appeal in this era of the conservative restoration.

We do not claim that all the supporters of charter schools are conservative. We do claim, however, that with few exceptions, supporters of charter schools have bought into the conservative worldview and political agenda. One of the intriguing social and political paradoxes of the educational reform movement from the 1980s to today is that conservatives embrace both deregulation and standards at the same time. While radical critics of conservatism have offered explanations as to why this seeming paradox is internally politically consistent, one does wonder if local control is really compatible with a national set of academic standards—as well as a national movement to evaluate students and schools against these standards.

Moreover, the cry for deregulation has never been entirely squared with the cry for local control or grassroots support for public education's remaining firmly in the hands of the public. Lest we forget, alternative education is not an invention of the right. Far from it. Americans have been resisting state schooling from its inception, particularly since the end of the nineteenth century when public education fundamentally took root in American communities and American conscience. Roman Catholics created their own mass and elite school system, social elites founded their own Anglophile schools in what amounted to a school enclosure movement, and "progressives" of all manner founded progressive schools that often claimed to be following the principles of John Dewey (often to his chagrin). In short, criticisms of public education did not begin in the 1980s.

If we view the charter school movement as a form of symbolic politics, there is little likelihood that we can explain its appeal by a single factor. Dissatisfaction with public education is far too simple an explanation for the rise of the charter school movement, because school reform movements have both obvious and non-obvious causes and expected and unexpected outcomes. Moreover, dissatisfaction with public education is nothing new. For us the non-obvious causes are hidden from view because they are part of the deep structure of American life. We see ourselves as social geologists digging down through each layer of explanation, until we arrive at the deepest structural explanation. In this chapter we examine the following explanations for the rise of the charter school movement:

- **Support for charter schools is politically expedient, thus appealing to a wide spectrum of politicians.**
- **Charter schools reflect the spirit of the times.** We are living in an era when the belief in markets, and quasi-markets, has reached near evangelical levels. This new "every man and woman a capitalist" ethos we describe as "populist elitism." In the last ten years we have seen the rise of the educational amateur. The press, in particular, has a public love affair with those well-intentioned but sometimes ill-informed heroes of education who believe that charisma will beat research and planning every time.
- **At a deeper level, there is a mismatch between the capacities and perspectives of most of public education and the emerging society.** Science and technology, in particular, are changing at an exponential rate, while schools change at a glacial rate. There is some truth to the claim that we are entering the twenty-first century with a nineteenth century school system. This is perhaps the root cause of the public's dissatisfaction with public education.
- **We are living through a period in which there is a popular perception that government is part of the problem—not part of the solution.** Nearly all political candidates campaign against the government, not for it. This anti-government sentiment has spilled over onto public education. Whereas public education was once the pride of America, it has been turned into a perfidious expression of state control. Books about the "public school monopoly"[1] have helped to create the public impression that "state" schooling is somehow un-American.

- **Closely associated with this attack on public education is a general political shift to the right in the United States.** This shift has several specific parts that will inform our discussion: the near-complete collapse of the left, the slow suicide of liberalism, the growth of a "third way" political movement that tends to blur political differences, and the growth of the new conservatism. The new conservatism has two dynamic political wings, market evangelism and fundamental religion. Both of these perspectives tend to view life through an ideological prism of material and spiritual rugged individualism. And lastly, the rewriting of recent American history by conservatives has led to the public perception that those who believe in and fight for social justice are somehow subversive and "un-American."

- **Educational credentials have traditionally been a major asset for most seeking upward mobility.** What do credentials mean in today's economy? We examine charter schools from this perspective and suggest that charter schools may benefit from an economy that is increasingly emphasizing performance as the criteria for employment or continued employment.

- **The rise of the right is accompanied by the closing of the social frontier.** Despite all the hoopla that surrounded the new economy, working class Americans are experiencing downward mobility and the traditional middle class is barely hanging on by the skin of their teeth. The amount of concentrated wealth in the United States has prevented upward mobility for the poor, the working poor, and the middle class. This is because we have become a "winner-take-all" society in which huge rewards are bestowed on a very few, leaving crumbs for the rest. For some, escaping to a charter school is a way out of this dilemma; unfortunately, like most escape strategies, it is illusionary.

- **At the same time that the country is experiencing a radical shift of wealth upward, the political discourse has shifted from collective interest to identity politics.** Because the media tend to ignore structural dilemmas and emphasize topical issues, citizens (and that ever-decreasing subsector of citizens—voters) tend to view politics as a matter of taste and fashion. Do I like the candidate and will he or she support my particular pet cause? Charter schools are the educational expression of identity politics—"I want my child to go to school where the parents think as I do." Educational reform usually reflects major social trends; no industrialization, no mass education, no compulsory school system. The credentials of the industrial era seem out-of-place in the post-modern society of e-commerce and instant gratification. Today, society is changing at an exponential rate, while education lags further and further behind. We will examine some of the most significant trends and connect them to the deregulation movement and to charter schools in particular.

- **In the last twenty years, the market metaphor has come to dominate public discourse and public policy.** The belief that markets are more efficient in producing social goods and more just in the distribution of those goods has become the new conventional wisdom. This worldview leads to a conviction that privatizing public institutions is not only an inexpensive method of reform, but morally laudable. The privatization movement reflects a larger belief system that the private sector is more rational, more accountable, and more productive. We explore this belief in markets and privatization because while charter schools are "public," their ethos is based on market conceptions of how schools can improve through competition.

- **Last, because we are sociologists, we cannot leave an analysis of the charter school movement without relating it to the class system, particularly the class system that has evolved in the last thirty years.** Schooling is an expression of class relations; wealthy children have always received a different education than poor children. Class-based education influences not only what is studied, but also how it is studied and what the social consequences are for those who receive the "best" education—and for those who do not. When the chairman of the board of a major corporation sends his or her son or daughter to a local start-up storefront charter school instead of Choate or Groton, we may have to revise our argument. Charter schools appear to serve as escape routes in an educational system that recreates class relations with unerring and unnerving accuracy.

In the next pages we elaborate on these arguments.

Expediency

Imagine yourself as a young politician with high political aspira-
tions confronted with the "crisis" in education. Actually, the
schools in your district are reasonably good—at least the parents
thinks so. Yet, nationally, most Americans believe that public education is a mess; fashionable and well-published intellectuals are
claiming that the only way out of the educational crisis is to break
the "public school monopoly." Whether you are an old Democrat,
a new Democrat, a moderate Republican, a conservative Republican, or a Libertarian, you know one thing—to survive you must
embrace the market and distance yourself from government,
which is ironic because you foresee a career for yourself in government. Some of the most fashionable critics of public education are
calling for a complete deregulation of public education through
vouchers. And to increase the complications of your political calculations, you have a sizable constituency of Roman Catholics,
some of whom are active supporters of vouchers. On the other side
of the political equation are the teachers unions; they despise
vouchers—and they have deep pockets and long memories.

What do you do? Stand pat and be seen by the national party
and its leading ideologues as hopelessly backward looking; embrace vouchers and incur the wrath of the teachers unions; undermine the public schools in your district where the majority of parents give their schools high marks?

Fortunately, there is a way out. It is called charter schools. It is
the perfect compromise. Why? Because is has deregulation sex appeal without going to the extreme of vouchers. Second, the teachers unions are supportive or indifferent. Third, while it doesn't reward the Catholic Church, it doesn't punish it either. Fourth, it is
an opportunity to do something about the educational scandal of
how poor children are schooled at no extra cost. It's a very expedient and cheap solution to a dangerous political situation. If you
vote for charter school regulation there is no organized block of
constituents to oppose you and there may be multiple photo ops as
charter schools are opened.

The Rise of the Educational Amateur
and the Populist Elitist

In an era when the market reigns supreme, it is not unexpected that a new social type will be born. Each era creates its ideal social type: the Roman citizen, the medieval knight, the solid and serious French bourgeois citizen, and the twentieth century fun-loving narcissist. Of course, each era has other social types that appeal to subgroups within larger groups: the monk at the time of the knight, the revolutionary at the time of the bourgeois citizen, the deeply religious at the time of the self-indulgent. This social dialectic captures the flow forward and backward across generations as values embodied in people compete in the marketplace of ideas and ideal types. Sometimes types blend together to form a new social type, a social type in tune with an emerging new era. In the last few years, a new social type has emerged to represent our new ideological atmosphere. It is the "you can do well and do good" type. This we call the populist elitist. In fact, most of our public figures, and those who are prominent in the charter school movement, are of this type. They merge two seemingly contradictory social views. On the one hand, they are fervently supportive of the common man and woman and believe in providing unlimited opportunities for all. Populism is as old as Jacksonian democracy and is expressed in countless attacks on America's cultural and political elites. The anti-intellectualism in American life has been amply documented. Yet, the new populism is almost entirely composed of elites, whether they are intellectuals, high-ranking politicians, or those who are, frankly, just wealthy.

When C. Wright Mills wrote of the power elite almost fifty years ago, he imagined and described a small group at the top that controlled the important levers of social, political, and economic power.[2] This power elite ran the show and made little pretense of being devoted to the common man or democracy. Just as war is too important to be left to the generals, democracy is too important to be left to the voters. The power elite tended to live in certain expensive neighborhoods, send their children to elite schools, and have access to power through their positions at the top of the economic, political, cultural, and military hierarchy. The new power elite are less stuffy than the old power elite, but no less ambitious for control.

By now, most of us are aware of how concentrated wealth—1 percent of Americans own 56 percent of the wealth—has affected public life and public institutions. Elected officials are forced to court wealth to finance their campaigns, lobbyists pour millions of dollars into politicians' pockets to gain favor and to influence public policy and legislation, and public discourse has largely been reduced to watching TV news and cable TV shows. The detachment of Americans from the institutions of democracy seems remarkably complete. Do we dare survey the citizens of any large state to determine if they know the names of their representatives and senators? Economic elitists have so successfully gained the heights in American life that most of us have forgotten, or never knew, that in a democracy, decisions are to be made by the people through their elected representatives, *not* through deals cut by contributors and public servants.

There was a time when elites ignored public education; after all, that's the point of private education—avoidance of the common. But the new power elite derives considerable political strength and social protection by associating itself with those "less fortunate, at-risk." Co-optation is a far more subtle and elusive form of social control than open conflict. How ironic that elites described earlier in this book should lead the way in calling for school deregulation at the very time when they educate their children in private schools or in suburban schools that amount to little more than private schools operating with public funding. Of course, some of the new elite hope to personally benefit from deregulation by sharing in investments in educational for-profit companies, hence, the contradiction of charter school companies. What originated as a liberal civil movement became a corporate movement led by the elites in the name of helping the poor.

The general social type ("do well and do good") became distilled into a specific ideal type—the educational amateur. Private education has a deep faith in the educational amateur. In fact, it is almost a prerequisite for promotion that a young private school teacher has little or no "professional" education training. The idea behind this worldview is that character, breeding, and exposure to elite education will beat commonplace professional development every time. What you know is less important than your background and whom you know. Up to the early 1990s this cult of the amateur was confined to private education; the growth of populist elitism has spread this belief to the public sector. In fact, almost the entire educational privatization movement is fueled by a skepticism concerning professional education.

Clearly, the charter school movement is founded on the belief that good will and hard work are prerequisites for success. Americans have always placed a great deal of their hope on heroes. Heroes are our favorite social type. The mass media, in particular, is enamored with heroes on the playing field, in business, and on the screen. The blur between real heroes and celebrity heroes is so great that many Americans believe that movie stars John Wayne and Ronald Reagan really *were* war heroes.

The idea of structure rubs a lot of Americans the wrong way. In the land of the rugged individual, there is little positive sentiment for collective action or structural explanations of progress. Society itself is a collection of individuals, a place where ascriptive characteristics such as class, race, and gender as collective identities are strongly resisted by most of the public. Most Americans believe they are middle class, a position won and maintained by individual effort. Structure sounds vaguely socialistic and, hence, the enemy of freedom, the supreme goal of individual striving. By attaching the heroic figure to school innovation, the charter school acquires the mantel of the pioneer struggling against long odds and thus finds its way into the hands and minds of many journalists who are eager for a good human relations story.

The Educational Mismatch

It is often repeated, but nonetheless a truism, that one of the fundamental challenges facing public education today is that its nineteenth century origins are still very much with us. Public education is still organized into grade configurations, student promotion is still based primarily on age, most classrooms are traditional and rely on teacher talk, assessment tends to be based on batch-sorting, and the curriculum itself is remarkably traditional—and for post-modern students, may be quite boring. If a school inspector from 1902 were to come back to life and visit schools in 2002, he or she would most likely find little that was unexpected or radically different. Schools remain steadfastly bureaucratic and, like the proverbial aircraft carrier, very difficult to turn around.

At the same time, society has changed dramatically. Our economy has moved from an industrial base to a service base, our attitudes toward race, sexual orientation, and difference in general are more tolerant and experimental. Heterosexual marriage is not the exclusive basis for family organization, and life itself has been extended by several decades over the last century.

Politically and militarily, the twentieth century saw the United States emerge as the global power, especially after World War II. For some, this increasing world presence signaled the viability of the American Dream for all people; for others, the expansion of the United States' power around the globe looks remarkably like an empire. In the last half of the twentieth century, American multinational corporations became huge, dominating the domestic and world economy. This rise of business is accompanied by a decline in the power of labor unions and the emergence of Washington, D.C., as a world capital and the epicenter of international politics.

Perhaps the most striking change, however, was in the realm of science and technology. At the turn of the nineteenth century, few people used automobiles and communication relied on the printed word. The vast majority of Americans engaged in farming or other agricultural pursuits and communicated with each other, if at all, through letters. Today, people can communicate instantly, send data at the stroke of a key, and speak to and see each other anywhere in the globe. Television has transformed the way we see, think, and perhaps feel. Advances in science are even more spectacular. We can map the human genome and measure the time from the beginning of the universe. Medical breakthroughs are prolonging life and enabling us to overcome some of the diseases that have been the scourge of humanity for centuries. In short, we are living in a new era.

Thus, the contrast between our antique school system and our evolving society is truly striking. To some degree, the charter school movement is an attempt to capture the future. By breaking the mold of traditional schools, the charter school movement leads us to a more innovative, future-oriented form of schooling. In theory, parents can escape the nineteenth century school system and choose a new, modern school. Whether or not charter schools are a true bridge between the past and the future is a question that has yet to be fully resolved.

Anti-Government Attitudes

Certainly, the charter school movement is an expression of the anti-government feelings so widely felt in the United States. Apparently, large segments of Americans resent the presence of government in their life. This resentment can reach extremes such as the far-right militia revolutionary groups that seek to undermine the government through terror. But most anti-government feelings are expressed by tax revolts and organized political campaigns around issues of the environment, health, and education. How truly representative these feelings are of the general popular sentiment is difficult to tell since these groups are so much more adamant than the general populace.

In the last twenty years, there has been a growing criticism of government as self-interested, slow moving, and inept. The anti-government coalition, if one can use this phrase, has targeted public education as the last great bastion of government ineptitude. Many authors, some independent and others associated with conservative think tanks and foundations, have gone so far as to say that private schools are more like common schools than are public schools! They make their argument as follows: Because of residential class and race segregation, most public schools are relatively homogeneous in terms of the demographic composition of their student bodies; public schools are not "melting pots." Private schools, on the other hand, are not tied to a particular neighborhood and can, therefore, draw students from various backgrounds. They believe that this is especially true of Roman Catholic schools; because of this, Catholic schools are more like common schools than public schools.

This position has several flaws: (1) The reason the Constitution separates church and state is because in a democracy "common" means—for all (such as the village commons), not just for members of one religion; (2) The researchers who study private schools have misrepresented the exclusive nature of private schools; contrary to their assertions, most private schools are educational enclaves designed to exclude groups whether it be for religious, social, or academic reasons; and (3) The idea that we would promote greater educational and social mobility by de-funding public education seems to fly in the face of common sense. Far closer to the point are equal funding for public schools and strategies for reducing class size.

Notwithstanding the shakiness of the anti-government argument in relation to education, there is little doubt that the deregulation and disestablishment movement has successfully convinced the mainstream media that public education is the enemy of social justice, not its supporter.

The Rise of the Right

Had the left and liberals remained strong and vital, probably none of these attacks on public education would have gotten far beyond the book and the chalkboard. The collapse of liberalism, in particular, has damaged the public sphere, including public schools. This demise might be called an assisted suicide, made possible by the conservative coalition, in particular by the religious fundamentalists' attack on "secular humanism" and the free marketers' attack on state planning or even state intervention on behalf of the economically and socially disadvantaged. For most marketers, the charter school solution is a weak solution because, for them, quasi-market solutions are like being quasi-pregnant. Yet, to switch metaphors, most deregulation advocates will take half of a loaf and support charter schools as a step in the right direction.

Since the 1980s American politics has drifted and is sometimes shoved increasingly rightward. The Reagan revolution altered the political discourse for a generation. The liberal worldview based on competing interests, mild government intervention, and a progressive tax code was turned upside down in the 1980s. Business became the dominant social, political, and economic interest group. Government intervention was rejected as making social problems worse, not better, and the tax code was rewritten in favor of the wealthy.

This revolt of the affluent is a striking historical phenomenon and has set the tone of public debate up to the present day. The school deregulation movement is part of this rightward turn. The core premise of school deregulation is that competition produces excellence, but government engineering produces mediocrity. It's unclear to us if this argument is a true belief or a cover story. Has competition empirically been shown to produce the economic cornucopia its advocates suggest? Most of the world lives in abject poverty. Is this because of insufficient capitalism or is it the result of the unequal distribution of resources? Whatever the truth about capitalism's contributions to social health or social sickness, there is little doubt that as an overarching ideology and worldview, it has triumphed in the latter part of the twentieth century and the early part of the twenty-first century.

History has a strange cunning and its events influence each other in unexpected ways; it is possible that the collapse of the Berlin Wall did more to legitimize the school choice movement than a thousand learned research projects. The dramatic exposure of Communism's failure to fulfill its number one mission—to dignify working men and women—opened the ideological field for those who posit that individualism left unrestrained will create a better and freer society. The failure of Communism, and by extension socialism, casts a shadow over all public institutions. Public schools became "state" schools and Catholic schools became "common schools." Who wants to send their child to a state school—it sounds totalitarian and a place for brainwashing of the Soviet sort. The mind of the right is complex—it places freedom and liberty as the core of all social activities, fears those that are different, and loathes authority except its own. Very often the right revels in military glory, jingoism, and red, white, and blue patriotism. Ambiguity and paradox are not the stuff of right-wing thinking.

Clearly, public education as a state monopoly is bound to catch the attention of the right; from the right's perspective, it is scary to send your child to a state school that forces him or her to study "secular humanism." Better to remove the child all together and home school. If home schooling is not possible, better to send your child to a private school or, even better, send him or her to a free public school that is not controlled by the heavy hand of the quasi-socialist school system and teachers' unions.

Thus, the school choice movement is far more than a school policy alternative devised by thoughtful policy wonks and earnest school practitioners. It is a conservative social movement. The charter school movement has its liberals and ex-radicals, but the juice that keeps it going is from the right. Two recent studies by the U.S. Department of Education make this point clearly. According to the reports, charter schools are changing school districts and giving new meaning to the word accountability. Yet, the evidence amounts to anecdotes and hearsay and signals to the discerning reader a simple message, "Don't mess with charter schools."

Redefining Credentialism

Sociologist Randall Collins has demonstrated convincingly that what is learned in school isn't half as important for the transmission of privilege as the simple fact of graduation.[3] Employers virtually never ask perspective employees what they studied in school or even how well they did; the simple fact of graduation signals to the employer that the applicant has the right sort of social characteristics to be successful and will accept the authority of the employer. Graduation from a socially elite secondary school and college is a genuine door-opener into the power suites of America. This is the "chartering" effect of schools discussed by sociologist John Meyer and others.[4] Above and beyond our personal characteristics and achievements, our education is a credential to be used in the economic, cultural, and political marketplaces.

All of this was undoubtedly true in the industrial era. Heavily bureaucratic and positional, the industrial office and school filled slots with people with the most reliable method of sorting and selecting—school credentials. But in the post-industrial era, where bureaucracy accounts for less and performance accounts for more, school credentials start to count for less. The owner of a company creating on-line virtual reality instruction is more likely to hire the "unschooled" but hip and technologically risk-taking adolescent than the fully credentialed college-bred applicant, because in the competitive world of e-commerce, few people care if you went to Yale. But they really care if you can make money. In this sense, our society is getting more and more like show business or sports—talent is what is what matters, not academic performance.

This trend favors the deregulation movement because traditional educational labeling accounts for less, giving the less well-known schools a chance to succeed and attract parents. It probably still helps to graduate from a prestigious public or private secondary school, but it is not a prerequisite for admission to a top college—or a top job. Perhaps later in one's career, as he or she enters the managerial ranks, the "old school tie" might help—but not too much. If Bill Gates has taught us nothing else, it's that in the post-industrial era, performance is the key to success. And in a winner-take-all economy, educational credentials account for little.

Thus sending your child to a relatively unknown charter school may not hurt his or her chances for mobility. It might even help, as college admissions offices are as susceptible as anyone when it comes to a media-hyped view of reality. Getting a few students from an urban charter school signals that the college is socially conscious and supportive of innovation. In fact, the pipeline from the academic charter school to the private college is likely to become filled because, like other small schools, charter schools can get into the college admissions game easily and succeed. Choosing an alternative public school may prove to be a smart career move. Thus, as home-schoolers (zero credentials) are in demand by colleges, charter school graduates will also be in demand.

The Closing of the Social Frontier

The movement to deregulate public education coincides with a period in American history when social mobility slowed and even regressed. If we recall that the primary justification for financing public education is to create a level playing field for all American children, the news that public education primarily recreates the social order is shocking. Public education is stratified in the same configuration as society is stratified. If we know a student's SAT score, we can with reasonable accuracy predict his or her family's income and perhaps wealth. In a world of imperfect measures, the SAT stands out as being able to identify a student's class background, not perfectly, of course, but with exceeding reliability and accuracy.

For decades Americans have been under the impression that here in the United States, individuals can get ahead and raise their social status through education, hard work, and talent. Some do, and of course, the super-novas catch our attention. But on balance, one's origin predicts one's destination. Large leaps in status are very rare; most mobility is between the upper working class and the lower middle class. The daughter of a plumber's assistant can become a teacher by attending a college. But for her to become a doctor would be difficult. And to become the head of a publishing firm, or a U.S. senator, is very unlikely.

Moreover, the middle class in the last twenty years has suffered considerable downward mobility. The real value of their wages has declined relative to the others. An individual making $40,000 in today's world cannot create wealth without winning the lottery. In fact, it may be that the rising tide of anti-government sentiment we are experiencing is related to the blocked mobility of so many Americans. Movie stars and other celebrities may jam the airways with voyeuristic mobility pleasures, but in reality most of us are wage earners with virtually no possibility of escaping the fate of all wage earners: Be at work on time, respect authority, be at least competent in your assigned duties, and pray that social security will not be bankrupt when you retire. This blocked mobility is political dynamite. Not only does it breed resentments, it calls into question the American Dream. But the American Dream dies hard. It's our social glue, our shared secular religion, and our abiding faith in the future. Yet in the recesses of our hearts, we know that the American Dream is a fantasy for most people.

The school deregulation movement tries to capture the American Dream of unlimited opportunities. It says to the middle classes, "If you get a really good education, the good life is attainable. You can't get a good education in the state system, opt out and let your child attend a small mission-driven school where he or she will reach his or her potential and get a jump-start on the great American status race." Charter schools become safety valves to the ambitious and the angry who instinctively know that sending their sons and daughters to the high school down the block provides no mobility function unless they are great athletes or super test-takers. The idea of exit, even escape, animates much of the deregulation movement. As the escape valve of public discontent, charter schools—or rather the idea of charter schools—serve a social purpose for those who wish to preserve the social order. By offering a way out, charter schools ensure that the issue of social mobility through merit is at least partially disguised.

The Privatization of America and the Growth of the Market Metaphor

Private schools, private prisons, private communities, private roads, private clubs, private selves . . . and now privatizing public school. This impulse to remove public goods and services from the public sector has become stronger and stronger. This increasing sense of creating private worlds can be seen in a politics of personal identity rather than in a politics of social issues or causes.

Voters are less likely to vote their "class" interest than they are to vote their personal interest, whether it is concerning their pocketbooks or their sexual preferences. This withdrawal from public life and public commitments has lead to the private sector's taking over ever increasingly large parts of community and family life.

Is it really any wonder that in a country where many families find themselves at the fast-food outlet for the evening meal, they would also willingly send their children to "fast food" schools? The provision of social goods by private corporations has become so pervasive that we have become almost totally dependent on the multinational to provide our daily bread as well as our gourmet coffee. The marketing of mass products as though they were individually tailored to each consumer is the genius of the multinational corporation. Starbucks may feel like a cozy local coffee shop, but it's actually an international business. Politics is similar. After carefully studying surveys and focus groups, politicians fashion a political platform tailored to appeal to everybody individually, but to nobody as part of a larger group. Each of us has our own little customized political agenda and we vote accordingly.

In *Democracy on Trial*, political scientist Jean B. Elshtain wrote:

The joint property of various liberalisms and conservatisms, twentieth-century purveyors of progress as an ideology celebrated a world of endless growth, which meant, in practice, more and better consumerism. It was essential to move from the glorification of producer to the glorification of consumer because the conclusion was that under-consumption leads to declining investment. We want more and we want it now! All of life is invaded by the market and pervaded by market imagery. Perhaps we should not be too surprised that in America's inner cities, young people rob, beat and even kill one another to steal expensive sneakers and gold chains. Or that in America's suburbs, young people whose families are well off shun school and studies and community involvement to take part-time jobs to pay for extra consumer goods that their parents may loath to provide.[5]

Referencing the work of sociologist Alan Wolfe, she asks, "Why have we lost a sense of social solidarity, why have we given up our freedom to concentrated political and economic power, why have we allowed ourselves to become 'bounded in our little kingdoms of one.'"[6] To her mind, this dangerous state of affairs has resulted in the loss of civil society—the soil of democratic dispositions, sentiments, and convictions. Like Tocqueville, she reminds us that democratic institutions cannot bloom, flourish, and replenish themselves if their roots are cramped and shriveled by a society gone mad by consumerism and individualism. A culture of cynicism and victimization is poor nourishment to the democratic impulse. Much of the choice rhetoric is fueled by market analogies, which infer that competition is the conceptual keystone to educational renewal.

Much of what is written about markets is abstract and avoids the obvious. Markets are power systems; suppliers shape demand through advertisement, and the distribution of profits is upward to the owners and the managers. Ours is not an economy of "mom and pop" stores. Advanced capitalism is, if not monopolistic, highly centralized and cooperates with government. The social ethos of advanced capitalism could be described as an ideology of consumerism, which itself is an outgrowth of the bourgeois worldview, in which material acquisition is considered the primary social good. Simply put, individuals pursuing their own self-interest create a common good because, collectively, self-interest is a better arbiter of human affairs than "social engineering."

A 1989 White House workshop on school choice unabashedly connected school choice with the marketplace. Dennis Doyle, a senior research fellow at the Hudson Institute in Washington, D.C., and a workshop participant, summarized: "There is in the popular mind a vision of cut-throat competition, of profit-making buccaneers swashbuckling across the State, people who are . . . merciless, kind of *Atlas Shrugged*/Ayn Rand types. Well, there certainly is that type of competition, but there is competition which is closer to home . . . and that is the competition which emphasizes the supremacy of the consumer, consumer sovereignty, and that, in fact, is what competition is all about."[7] This eulogizing of the market has been given legitimacy by intellectuals and others working in such conservative foundations and think tanks as the American Enterprise Institute, the Heritage Foundation, the Hudson Institute, the Cato Institute, and the Manhattan Institute. In the last fifteen years, academics have published a small library of books extolling the efficacy and justice of markets and have been very successful in creating a political climate in which public institutions are put on the defensive and programs for public welfare are considered "part of the problem" rather than part of the solution.

Discussions about markets and quasimarkets applied to education generally fail to identify the actual characteristics of markets or the historical origins of the market worldview. Markets for goods are characterized by differentiated products, close-ended agreements to buy and sell, clear comparisons, and measurable marginal utility. The market for intellectual services, on the other hand, has undifferentiated products (that is, ideas, theories, and so on), open-ended agreements about the learning process, very few clear comparisons (the life of the mind is hard to quantify), and immeasurable marginal utility. Analogies between the market for goods and the market for ideas are misleading. There is a distinction to be made between commodity markets and social markets. We would further argue that the strengthening of the social marketplace is critical if the commodities marketplace is not to undermine the fabric of society. George Soros, the wealthy philanthropist, has written about the "capitalistic threat." He worries that the state in unfettered capitalism will become the gangster state. If marginal economic utility is the only human exchange that is socially sanctioned, then all other kinds of exchanges that make society essential and beneficial will become less credible, wither, and evaporate in history.

Virtually all societies recognize that there is an inherent tension between the individual and the group and that the just society keeps both in balance by tolerating individual expression but insisting on pro-social behavior. In the United States today, social marketplaces are very undeveloped and those that have developed are threatened by the larger economic society. Robert Putnam's book *Bowling Alone* is but one example of many books and articles discussing the loss of civil life in late-twentieth-century America.[8] It is not just an amusing social artifact to know, for instance, that 43 million more Americans watched the Super Bowl in January 1997 than voted in the presidential election of 1996. It is instructive to know that the average American watches more than six hours of television a day; one can only speculate how much of the average American's waking hours are spent looking at a screen, including a computer screen. The loss of a vibrant social market parallels the decay of urban life and with it the commitment to education for those in the bottom third of the class structure.

Class Reproduction and the Appearance of Mobility

Wealth creation and wealth distribution are the volatile intersection of economics and politics. When wealth is distributed "justly," there is a sense of social harmony. When the distribution of wealth is not perceived as just, a sense of disharmony prevails, leading to conflict. Most often this conflict is latent, buried under cultures that rely on compelling myths of social unity and religious myths of postmortem paradise. Sometimes conflict is manifest, leading to rebellion and on occasional revolution. Thus, the very heart of public philosophy and public policy is the management of property relations, the DNA of society. Property relations do not refer to what people own, but the social relationships that arise from ownership. Slave and master are social categories based on a relationship—and a claim of dominance by the master that has little to do with public displays of status. Similarly, the relationship of employee to employer is not based on consumption—both might own Cadillacs—but on the power of the employer over the employee's career.

At the group level, these power relations are crystallized and consolidated into "class" relations. The concept of class is common in Europe but missing from how most Americans think about society. The common perception is that we are a nation of individuals.

In fact, our belief in rugged individualism defines our national identity.

Race is a division that has torn apart the national fabric from its inception, but we avoid the idea of collective responsibility for racism; if anything, we tend to blame the victims and expect that African-Americans, as individuals, pull themselves up by their bootstraps. Other divisions tend to run along cultural lines and not structural lines. We find differences according to gender, sexual orientation, ethnicity, religion, and region, but most of these "differences" reflect the two Americas—one intensely inward looking and local, the other outward looking and cosmopolitan.

These cultural differences sometimes generate a lot of rhetoric and spilt ink, resulting in identity politics, but no major structural or political changes. On the subject of class, however, most mainstream media outlets, even the most respectable publishers, remain oddly silent, except perhaps to offer the public exciting little tidbits about the lifestyles of the rich and famous. Class—at the political, economic, and social levels—is thought of, if it is thought of at all, as another leftist attempt to throw cold water on the ongoing celebration of individualism and the deeply held belief that everybody can be a winner. Those who grumble about structural obstacles to success are naysayers who are probably eggheads anyway. Yet, even a cursory glance at society and the economy should sober us into a recognition that class is alive and well in the United States. In the last twenty years, class lines have become deeper, not shallower, resulting in a society that is deeply divided. One percent of the population owns 56 percent of the wealth. Ten percent owns 80 percent of the wealth. The concentration of wealth at the top has resulted in an 80/20 society. Eighty percent owns almost nothing, or nothing at all. Twenty percent owns virtually everything, resulting in a true concentration of power—the new elite controls business, entertainment, the news, and political life. Sociologists have examined the new class system and make fine distinctions between the new middle class, the old middle class, the professional class, and the ownership class. These studies are important and illuminating but can become a "forest for the trees" problem. What matters is the powerful predictor that if you are born poor, you will, in all likelihood, die poor. To weaken or disassemble this class structure would require the greatest reform effort in American history, equal to the effort to eliminate slavery during the Civil War. This reform is unlikely to happen under the present conditions. In a blame-the-victim society that encourages individual accumulation, most of our eyes are firmly focused on the individual prize, not on the collective good.

Seen in this light, it is difficult to imagine charter schools in any way reducing class differences, or providing class mobility. Ten thousand charter schools educating two million students (a very unlikely occurrence) would only result in more options for individuals, but do nothing to weaken the processes of educational reproduction. In fact, alternative schools may do well by some individuals, but may only reinforce class-based education by providing small escape hatches for relatively few students. Thus, charter schools are not likely to level the playing field in any significant way, but rather to indirectly reinforce the tilt of the playing field in favor of the already favored.

We begin this section by referring to our subtitle, "The Politics of Hope and Despair." Obviously, we are unconvinced that random acts of reform or the privatization of education will result in a just school system for all children. We do not question the motivation of those who found charter schools, and we fully recognize that many charter schools may be "good" schools. Any school that helps children should be applauded.

The charter school movement, however, is not likely to transform American education. It may even be a diversion. Our research shows that the educational impact of charter schools is surprisingly small. This low impact is attributable to several causes elaborated on earlier—all the way from the nature of schooling to the social and political context of education that speaks of achievement, but acts to stratify children and families. Moreover, the market metaphor for schooling turns out to be something of a paper tiger. Competition isn't what makes schools great—*people and resources* make schools great . . . and also make them vulnerable to failure.

Marketization is an outward-directed reform—it focuses on external forces as the shapers of schools. We believe that real reform comes from inward-directed reform. Schools begin with certain core values that are shared across school and class boundaries and are held true, through thick and thin. Genuine reform requires planning, resources, and a unifying system of beliefs. In our brief Postscript, we touch on what we believe would constitute a just and productive school system.

POSTSCRIPT:
The Goodness of America—
An Education for Democracy

What do American children need today if they are to become citizens of the world tomorrow? A child born today could well live into the next century: It is almost beyond our imaginations to grasp what changes will occur in a child's lifetime and what challenges he or she will face. We are living during an epoch of exponential change; the world of our parents does little to predict the world of our children and grandchildren. Yet, we continue to tinker with our nineteenth-century school system. We look backward when we should look forward. When we think of the future we envision students with deep pride, open, inquiring minds, and moral courage. We envision students who resist rigid ideologues and fantastic escapist beliefs; an open and just society cannot exist without open minds and open hearts. Deep feelings, however, without critical analysis, imagination, knowledge, and determination can lead to solipsism, personal entropy, and social decay.

To develop deep feelings that are guided by ethical maturity and judgment requires curiosity, empathy, attachment, and accomplishment. Curiosity suggests inquiry; empathy requires tolerance; attachment needs safety; and accomplishment measures growth. Inquiry, tolerance, safety, and growth are the basis of an educated democracy.[1]

Mohandas Gandhi once identified the seven social sins: politics without principle, wealth without work, commerce without morality, pleasure without conscience, education without character, science without humility, worship without sacrifice. If we take the "out" from "without," we have a series of positive statements about the core values of the curriculum of the future. We should worry less that every child clears some imaginary age-graded hurdle and worry more that by the time of a child's graduation from high school he or she has internalized the core values of personal integrity and communal responsibility. Of course, children are not machines, as the standards movement suggests; they are volatile, complicated, and paradoxical. Education is never linear.

Education is not a product to be swallowed without reflection and struggle, nor is it information poured into an awaiting, but empty, brain. Education is a path to knowledge and wisdom. To be real, education is always personal, passionate . . . and difficult. To grow requires effort, persistence, and sacrifice. Education is creative and continuous and is meant to save psychic lives by lighting the cranial fire that is our species' mark of genius. Education is the opposite of training, regimentation, and standardization.

Not only is education deeply personal, it is inescapably political. As Aristotle noted, we are political animals. Our brains are products of social relations, social intrigue, and social bonding. Education is not a cloud floating above the earth of real life. It is real life, and real life is always a contest between competing interests, competing beliefs, and competing needs. This potential for discord can only be softened and resolved by a free and universal public education system because public schools are the "commons" upon which we agree to protect our children and to resolve our differences peaceably. Abstract discussions of curriculum removed from the needs of society are bound to fall in the hands of researchers, pundits, and educational speculators because they face no requirement to provide an education for justice and an education for an American vision of the future.

CURRICULUM AS STEWARDSHIP

What kind of curriculum would ignite the natural genius of children and promote inquiry, tolerance, safety, and growth? What kind of curriculum would enable children to become ethically mature as adults and join with others to create a strong and good America and a just global society? In this section, we suggest a curriculum based on stewardship in at least two senses—stewardship of children's growth and stewardship of an education for democracy. The design principles below are the conceptual scaffolding for a school system that promotes democracy. (These principles were previously published by Cookson in 2001).[2]

Design Principle One: Public education must be free and universal, accessible to all children

This principle seems self-evident, but the logic of school deregulation runs counter to this concept of free universal access. Market-driven reform either exploits scarcity or creates scarcity; in the strict sense there is no "market" for education except insofar as demand is created by the state or by individuals. The principle of universal access is the bedrock of public education. If, however, all children can attend public school and those schools are highly variable in terms of resources, pedagogical talent, and extracurricular support, what does such a right mean in practice?

Design Principle Two: All children are entitled to equal educational opportunities regardless of their class, race, gender, residence, or learning differences.

Access without equality is something of a policy shell game. A genuine definition of equal educational opportunities suggests—or demands—that all children must be offered curriculum, teaching, and support that favors all rather than the few. De facto class and race segregation in the United States means that the delivery of high-quality education is uneven and skewed in favor of the privileged.

Design Principle Three: Educational advancement based on family wealth must cease within schools and between schools.

But how does one stop educational advancement based on family wealth? We suggest the following: abolish tracking, equalize resources, prepare students to learn at high standards, and construct assessment instruments that test curricular competency rather than cultural capital. We know that the higher the collective class background of a student body, the greater the educational opportunities. Privilege undermines merit and when privilege allows for uneven competition, the basis of equal educational opportunity is undermined.

While it is true that individuals and groups are at liberty to form their own schools, they are not at liberty to rob others of educational mobility. When my liberty becomes your disadvantage, I have a privilege disguised as a right. By allowing alternative school systems to compete with the public school system, the principle of public rights is undermined. Yet, we are willing to forego some public rights for the sake of individual liberty. This social and legal compromise, however, should not result in private rights operating in such a way as to overshadow public rights; attending a socially elite school should not result in special mobility privileges.

Design Principle Four: Curricula should reflect our core democratic values and respect for individual abilities, learning styles, and intellectual desires.

Perhaps the most shocking aspect of the current system is how it lays to waste so much talent. This wastage can be found in all schools, although it is the most intense in schools located in communities of concentrated poverty. How many paintings will never be painted because students do not receive encouragement or support? How many potential humanitarians become gangsters because their worth is denied? How many future scientists do we lose every year because whole categories of students are treated with contempt? We need schools that are societies in John Dewey's sense, and we need to ensure that social ethics and tolerance are as much a part of curriculum as reading and arithmetic. Core democratic values include tolerance and empathy, but they also include clear thinking, taking responsibility, and a willingness to accept compromise gracefully. It is said that democracy can only flourish when the values associated with a civil society are present. Civility and a deep respect for honest achievement are at the heart of a substantive democracy where judgment based on reason and fact prevails over socially engineered mass emotion. Power will always be present in group life. Power is an engine for change and for the social good when contained, focused, and limited. When it becomes self-reverential and absolute, it destroys the good.

Design Principle Five: The social organization of schools must be democratic.

Within education, democracy is more honored in the breach than in practice. Most schools are hierarchical and authoritarian, even more so than most businesses. As long as the authority structure of the school is top down and the real decisionmaking is in the hands of a few administrators, students will be socialized into a worldview that encourages them to view powerlessness as a fact of life and reinforces the apathy to which most people are susceptible. A democratically organized school begins with families and their children. Participation in meaningful decisionmaking is the sine qua non of democracy. If families have no voice in the life of a school, then the school will always be an obstruction to the natural flow of social communication. The distinction between administration and staff is a form of dominance that breeds withdrawal, apathy, and anger. Creating new forms of decisionmaking is the next challenge facing all schools, although one might refer back to John Dewey for useful guidance.

In the present system, many students learn all too quickly that they have no future because they cannot or will not play the game. Is it any wonder that they become self-destructive? Schools should be places of joy, community, and intellectual freedom. Marketized, sanitized knowledge is the polar opposite of the wildness of heart that fires all genuine learning.

Design Principle Six: Schools must be part of their communities.

One of the most shocking and depressing aspects of the anti-public school movement is its complete disregard for the value of the community and how schools can help to create community even in the most distressed neighborhoods. Schools should no longer be thought of as buildings; rather, they should be thought of as communication networks, reaching out to the whole world through technology and reaching out to the local community through sharing and service. Schools should take responsibility not only for developing inquiring minds but also for developing healthy bodies and strong egos.

THE GOODNESS OF AMERICA

There are 800,000 children in the United States today who are farm workers with no medical protection, very little schooling, and almost no hope of a better life. One quarter of our children live in poverty; our global economy depends on exploiting child labor around the world. A cool pair of running shoes was most probably made by a young child in Asia earning perhaps one dollar a day. She might be lucky—her sister may be a slave in the sex industry.

We Americans have a responsibility to ensure that as the world's strongest nation we stand firmly in solidarity with the weakest of the world and demand for them what we expect for ourselves. If we choose to be selfish, what will our grandchildren say of us, when the gasoline finally runs out, when a very small number of us owns most of the wealth, and when 50 percent of our children cannot read? Will they say we frittered away the greatest social experiment in history?

The investment we make in students today will result in a society prepared to meet the challenges of the future. For Americans, the future is full of dangers and opportunities. Imagine the United States in 2050 . . . how will we have resolved the complex ethical problems created by bioengineering? How will we balance economic growth with ecological sustainability? Will our economy continue to separate the winners from the losers, thus creating a divided society? Will we honor and appreciate diversity—or will race and ethnic conflict "Balkanize" us, driving us into warring factions?

The American Dream was not forged at polite academic seminars, by think tanks, or by conventional thinkers. It was forged by those who dared to dream of an egalitarian, free society, who were willing to put their lives on the line in order to make that dream come true. The spirit of rebellion is essential if we are to grow, question, and reach higher levels of understanding and action. Increasingly, the machine metaphor of education has captured the imagination of policymakers, politicians, and, alas, even of educators. Students are raw material inputs; schools, which assign each student a score, process them. The student then graduates as a graded product (like lumber) to be assigned to his or her status and occupational niche. Unfortunately, many important Americans champion this uninspiring view of education; an American education should not be about producing workers, it should be about educating citizens and developing leaders.

To our minds, American civilization is torn between two grand narratives. One narrative is based on manifest destiny, accumulation, and greatness. This is the America of the American eagle—

proud, imperious, and even merciless. This grand narrative contrasts with the narrative of goodness. This American story is based on community, simple but sound values, and a fierce loyalty to justice. This is the America of the log cabin and of Thanksgiving. If we pursue the narrative of greatness, our children will become economic and military warriors, blinded by pride of victory and the struggle for dominance. If we help them learn the goodness narrative, they will create a just, humane civilization, as the founders of the Republic intended. Our young people deserve to live in a peaceful, bountiful world where intellectual adventure is more exciting than violent video games and sharing is more satisfying than consuming. Our children deserve an education worthy of their talent, hope, and goodness.

Clearly, we do not believe that public education should be deregulated in order to save it. During the war in Vietnam, some American policymakers believed that Vietnam had to be destroyed in order to save it. This was a dangerous and destructive policy that resulted in a grand failure. The effort to deregulate public schools will also be a grand historical failure. It is the equivalent of wishful thinking, or of expecting miracles.

We believe that to strengthen public education we ought to move away from fragmentation to unity, from randomness to systems thinking, and from hyper-individualism to a sense of attachment and belonging. If we are to succeed, we must build a system of schools that are animated with a sense of justice, and not wait for history to unfold and possibly engulf us. To expect miracles is to invite another fifty years of educational failure and social conflict.

APPENDIX

The following charter school application is taken from the Charter Schools Institute of the State University of New York's Charter Schools Application Kit, 3rd Edition.

The Charter Schools Institute of the State University of New York is one of three chartering entities in New York State, each of which has its own application and related materials.

This application would have been used by entities wishing to submit a charter school application for the Fall 2001 review cycle. Applications for future review cycles will be revised to reflect a constant process of improvement.

We have selected this application to illustrate the complexity of the charter school application process—and to provide readers with a first-hand look at the depth of planning that must go into the development of a charter school application.

CHARTER SCHOOL APPLICATION

TRANSMITTAL FORM AND COVER SHEET

Working Name of Charter School: _____

Applicant Contact: _____   _____
                        Print or type name   Signature

APPLICANT CONTACT INFORMATION

Mailing Address: _____

Telephone: _____

Facsimile: _____

E-mail: _____

Partner Organization (if any): _____

Contact (name/phone#): _____

SCHOOL SUMMARY

First year grade levels to be served: _____

First year targeted enrollment: _____

Location (school district): _____

COMPLETED APPLICATIONS MUST BE SUBMITTED TO:
Charter Schools Institute
State University of New York
74 North Pearl Street, 4th Floor, Albany NY 12207
Telephone: (518) 433-8277; Facsimile: (518) 427-6510
E-Mail: charters@sysadm.suny.edu
www.newyorkcharters.org

FOR OFFICE USE ONLY:

Received by: _____

Date Received: _____

I. ESTABLISHMENT AND SCHOOL DESIGN

1. **Provide the name of the proposed charter school.**

    Please note the following in responding to Request No. 1.

    .. The name of the school must by law include the term "charter school" and cannot include the name of a for-profit business or corporate entity. [§ 2851(2)(k)]

    .. If you are awarded a charter, you must use the full name of the charter school (as it appears in response to this Request). You may wish, therefore, to take this into account when considering how long the name of your school should be.

    > **Submit your response to Request No. 1 as Attachment 1.**

2. **Provide the name of each applicant. If you are applying as a single applicant, include your home address, telephone number(s) (home and office), facsimile number and e-mail address. If there is more than one applicant, you must then designate one applicant as the contact person for the application and provide the contact information set forth above for that individual. In addition, provide background information for each applicant, including whether he or she is a teacher, parent, school administrator, and/or community resident and if he or she would be a member of the charter school's board of trustees.**

    Please note the following in responding to Request No. 2.

    .. Only individuals who are teachers, parents, school administrators or community residents are eligible to serve as applicants to establish a charter school. [§ 2851(1)] An application for a charter school can be submitted by one or more of these eligible individuals. The Charter Schools Institute interprets the term "community resident" to mean an individual who resides either in the school district in which the school is to be located or who resides in geographic proximity to the proposed location of the school. Note that in New York City, the school district comprises all five boroughs.

    .. It is preferred that the background information that is to be provided for each applicant be in resume form. In all cases, and in whatever format, such background information must include, at a minimum, the applicant's educational and employment history. In addition, the background information should indicate that the applicant is at least eighteen years of age. [§ 2851(2)(m)]

    .. Organizations and entities, whether for-profit or not-for-profit, cannot serve as applicants, though they can submit an application in conjunction with eligible applicants (see Requests Nos. 8 and 9, below). [§ 2851(1)]

    .. The name and work phone number (or home number if no other number is given) of the contact person will be made available to school districts and the media. The contact information should be the same as the contact information provided on the Application

Transmittal Sheet. The Transmittal Sheet will be the first page of your Application. See the Instructions for further details.

.. *During the course of the application review process, the Charter Schools Institute may require a set of fingerprints for each applicant for the purpose of obtaining a state and federal criminal records check. [§ 2852(4)] The Institute, at the appropriate time, will send to the applicants a blank set of non-criminal fingerprint cards; unsolicited fingerprints sent to the Institute will be returned to the sender.*

Submit your response to Request No. 2 as Attachment 2.

3.   **Provide the anticipated opening date for the charter school (month/year).**

Please note the following in responding to Request No. 3.

.. *Most applicants automatically seek an opening date for the following September. While the great majority of applicants who have done so (and who have been awarded charters) have been successful in opening the school by their projected date, many of them have also indicated that they would have greatly benefited from a planning year. Accordingly, you may want to give thought, if you are applying in the summer of 2001, to seek an opening in September 2003, rather than September 2002. In this way, you will have more time, once chartered, to plan for your opening, including recruiting a school director and staff and developing in greater detail the policies and procedures of your school. The Institute strongly urges you to consider seeking a planning year and, at a minimum, discussing this issue with successful charter school applicants, technical resource providers in New York State and/or the Charter Schools Institute.*

Submit your response to Request No. 3 as Attachment 3.

4.   **Provide the requested initial term of the charter, which in no case is to exceed 5 years.**

Please note the following in responding to Request No. 4.

.. *A charter cannot exceed five years in length. [§ 2851(2)(p)] However, if approved, a charter can be renewed for additional five-year terms. [§ 2851(4)] Because the charter is for a definite term, it is called a "provisional charter." While you can request a shorter term for the charter than the maximum of five years, the Institute does not recommend that you do so. A shorter term will make it difficult for the charter school to report, as it is required by law to do, on the progress it has made in achieving its stated educational goals. [§ 2851(4)(a)]*

Submit your response to Request No. 4 as Attachment 4.

5.   **Provide for each year of the charter that you are seeking, the grades that the school would serve, the number of students to be served in each grade, the number of children expected in each class, and the total number of enrolled students. If providing a kindergarten, please indicate the minimum age that the school will require a child to have attained to be eligible for enrollment.**

Please note the following in responding to Request No. 5.

..   *A charter school is required by law to serve at least one of the grades 1 through 12. [§ 2854(2)(c)]*

..   *In addition to serving at least one of the grades 1 through 12, a school may (but is not required to) offer a kindergarten. [§ 2854(2)(c)]*

..   *If a school offers a kindergarten, such program must be open to all children otherwise eligible to attend who attain the age of five by December 1st of the year in which they first attend kindergarten. [§ 3202(2)] In other words, if you plan to open in September 2002, you cannot restrict admission to students who will turn five by, for example, the first day of school; rather you must allow all children to apply who will turn five by or before December 1, 2002.*

..   *Unless the school serves a geographically remote region, or presents some other compelling reason, the school must enroll a minimum of fifty students at a single site by the <u>second</u> year of its operation. [§ 2851(2)(i)] If you plan on serving less than fifty children at a single site in any but your first year of operation and you believe that your school would qualify for an exemption, please contact the Institute to discuss this issue. An application that seeks to serve less than fifty children at a single site in any but the first year, and does not provide a compelling reason or a showing of geographical remoteness, cannot be considered for approval.*

..   *In indicating how many children are to be in each class, i.e., your class size, you may wish to indicate a range, rather than a precise number. For instance, you may wish to say that your ideal number would be, for example, 20 students, but that staffing constraints, allowances for children held back or advanced a grade, etc., may require you to exceed that limit to a maximum of 23. It is important to remember that, if you are approved, your response, as your other responses, will set the terms under which the school is to operate unless the term (if material) is amended.*

> Submit your response to Request No. 5 as Attachment 5.

6.   **Provide the rationale for choosing to serve the grades and number of students in each grade and in the school as a whole. In addition, if you are planning to add grades or expand enrollment in the second or subsequent years of your charter, please explain the rationale for your growth plan.**

Please note the following in responding to Request No. 6.

.. *One of the hallmarks of charter schools is that they have the choice to determine what grades they serve and how many students in each grade. Accordingly, charter schools come in all sizes and many serve a different set of grades than a district public elementary, middle or secondary school. Whatever your choice – large or small, a few grades or a complete K-12 program, no growth or rapid growth in subsequent years – you should be able to provide a coherent rationale for having made that choice.*

Submit your response to Request No. 6 as Attachment 6.

7. (a) Indicate whether you have submitted a substantially similar application to another charter entity simultaneous with submission of this application. If so, provide the name of the charter entity, the date the application was submitted and the status of the application.

Please note the following guidance in responding to Request No. 7(a).

.. *Simultaneous submission constitutes a substantially similar application with substantially similar applicants, where such application remains under review by another charter entity with formal action pending by that charter entity.*

Submit your response to Request No. 7(a) as Attachment 7(a).

(b) If you have previously applied for a charter from another charter entity and it was denied, provide a copy of the letter from the charter entity stating the reasons the application was denied.

Submit your response to Request No. 7(b) as Attachment 7(b).

8. If you are filing the application in conjunction with a college, university, museum, educational institution, or a not-for-profit corporation with 501(c)(3) status under the Internal Revenue Code, please provide the information below for each such entity. If, on the other hand, you are filing this application in conjunction with a for-profit entity or a not-for-profit management company, and you are not applying in conjunction with any other of the entities described above, you may indicate that Request No. 8 is not applicable and proceed directly to Request No. 9. If you are not filing in conjunction with any entity, please so indicate in your responses to Requests Nos. 8 and 9 and proceed to Request No. 10.

.. name of the organization;

.. a letter of intent or commitment from a bona fide representative of the partner organization indicating that the organization is undertaking the partnership and the terms and extent of the undertaking;

.. the name of a contact person for the partner organization;

.. **the address, phone number, facsimile number, and e-mail of such contact person for the partner organization; and**

.. **a description of the nature and purpose of the school's partnership with the organization.**

Please note the following in responding to Request No. 8.

.. *The Charter Schools Institute uses the terms "partner" or "partner organization" to describe those entities in conjunction with which you are permitted to file a charter school application.*

.. *The letter of intent or commitment that you are required to provide from each partner organization must specify any services (for a fee or otherwise) or financial assistance that the partner has agreed to provide and that you have represented will be provided. If you represent that the school will be receiving a service for free or at a reduced rate from the partner organization, the letter from the partner must so indicate. If the partner does not provide a firm commitment, it will be assumed that either (i) a market rate will apply for such services (and the budget that you submit will be recalculated accordingly) or (ii) the service will not be provided.*

> *For example: if you elsewhere claim in the application that tutors will be provided by a university partner on a volunteer basis, and those tutors are a component of your remedial education program, the university partner must provide a firm commitment to provide such tutors on such basis. If this commitment is not provided, the Institute's financial analysts will recalculate the school's budgeted expenses to account for the service at the prevailing market rate or the Institute will review the proposed remedial program with the assumption that the university partner's tutors will not be provided.*

.. *In the past, the Institute has received applications that, at first glance, contain an impressive array of partners, many of them well-known institutions. However, on examination, many of those partners have not provided any evidence that they will supply any services to the school or that the limited services that they have indicated a willingness to provide are anything but peripheral to the school's mission and goals. Accordingly, in the Institute's experience, an applicant is better served by submitting an application in conjunction with only those entities that are committed to providing a substantial and tangible benefit to the proposed charter school. Indeed, in the eyes of the application reviewers, an applicant's credibility may suffer when he or she provides a list of partners that add little or nothing to the proposed school. In other words, quality, not quantity is the key.*

.. *Not every relationship that the school might have with community organizations requires that those organizations be identified formally as partners. For instance, if you plan on frequent field trips to local museums, those museums need not file an application in conjunction with you. It is sufficient to simply note, for instance in your curriculum, that you will use the resources that those entities normally supply to schools.*

> Submit your response to Request No. 8 as Attachment 8.

9. (a) If the charter school would be established in conjunction with a for-profit entity (including but not limited to a management company) or a non-profit management company, then please provide the name of such entity and specify the extent of the entity's participation in the management and operation of the school. As part of such discussion, please include the following:

    .. a term sheet indicating at a minimum, the fees to be paid by the proposed school to the management company, the length of the proposed contract, the terms for the contract's renewal and all provisions for termination; and

    .. copies of the last two contracts that the management company has executed with operating charter schools (in New York or other states) and, if applicable, the status of those charter schools' application for tax-exempt status under section 501(c)(3) of the Internal Revenue Code;

> Submit the "term sheet" required by Request No. 9(a) as Attachment 9(a).

> Submit the two management contracts
> required by Request No. 9(a) as Exhibit A.

(b) Please explain how and why the entity was selected.

Please note the following guidance in responding to Request No. 9(b).

    .. *The Institute is particularly interested in the specific steps that you took in arriving at your decision to file an application with a management company or other for-profit entity. If you are filing in conjunction with a management company, please provide a description of the due diligence that you conducted on the management partner selected and the degree of "comparison shopping" in which you engaged prior to making your selection. Boilerplate, unsupported statements to the effect that the management partner selected was the best candidate will not allow the application reviewers to effectively evaluate your response.*

> Submit your response to Request No. 9(b) as Attachment 9(b).

(c) If Requests Nos. 9(a) and 9(b) are applicable to your application, then provide all of the following information. If not applicable, please so note and proceed to Request No. 10.

    .. evidence that the corporate entity is authorized to do business in New York State;

    .. the number of schools the entity presently manages (if any) and the location of those schools;

    .. the length of time the entity has been in business;

.. the most recent annual report of the entity; and

.. a description or summary reports of student achievement results in schools managed by the entity.

Please note the following in responding to Request No. 9(c).

.. *If the school proposes to locate in a district with a significant number of children who receive free or reduced price lunches, the management partner will be expected to provide student achievement results for students in schools with which it is associated that are disaggregated between students who receive free or reduced lunches and those who do not.*

> Submit your response to Request No. 9(c) as Exhibit B.

II. SCHOOL MISSION AND SUMMARY

10.   **Develop and attach the mission statement for the proposed charter school.**

Please note the following in responding to Request No. 10.

.. *In responding to Request No. 10, applicants must review carefully the guidance regarding charter school mission statements that is contained in the Institute's Guidelines for Writing Charter School Accountability Plans (the "Accountability Plan Guide"), which is included in the Appendix of the Application Kit. The Accountability Plan Guide is also available on the Institute's web site. As you will see from reading the relevant parts of the Accountability Plan Guide, your mission statement should be clear and precise. Your mission statement should (in one or two sentences) indicate what the school intends to do, for whom, and to what degree. Some schools also use their mission statement to (briefly) address how they will accomplish these things if methodology is a particularly important part of their vision.*

.. *As you will also notice, and is the case with all sections of the Accountability Plan (which you will be asked to develop if chartered), your mission statement should be written for a general audience. Avoid jargon and technical terminology— parents and members of the community who wish to know more about the school should be able to read the mission statement and get a clear sense of your school and its vision. A mission statement that focuses on core elements and sets priorities will remind readers that you are responsible for following through on a very specific set of promises and that some aspects of school performance are more important than others.*

> Submit your response to Request No. 10 as Attachment 10.

11.   Provide an **"Executive Summary"** for the proposed charter school. The Executive
       Summary should include the following elements:

    .. *a detailed explanation of why you are seeking to open a public charter school, including why
       the charter school is necessary at this time and in the proposed area of location;*

    .. *an explanation, supported by concrete examples, of what the proposed school would do more
       effectively from the schools that are now serving the target population and how the school
       would be able to accomplish its goals;*

    .. *a brief description of the proposed school's education program and philosophy; and*

    .. *a description of how that program would implement one or more of the following purposes:*

        – *improve student learning and achievement;*

        – *increase learning opportunities for all students, including, in particular, expanded
          learning opportunities for children "at-risk" of academic failure;*

        – *encourage use of different and innovative teaching methods;*

        – *create professional opportunities for teachers, school administrators, and other
          personnel;*

        – *provide parents and students with expanded choices in the types of educational
          opportunities that are available within the public school system; and*

        – *institute a change from rule-based to performance-based accountability systems for
          meeting measurable student achievement results.*

    > Submit your response to Request No. 11 as Attachment 11.

III. ACADEMIC PROGRAM, STANDARDS, CURRICULUM & ASSESSMENT

12. (a) Provide a copy of the proposed school's calendar in the first year of its operation. The
        calendar must indicate the number of days of instruction that the school will offer.

    (b) Provide a daily schedule of the periods of instruction, i.e., academic subjects, recess or
        recreation, study periods, and length of the school day, including start time and dismissal
        time for each grade that you are to serve during the term of the provisional charter.

    Please note the following requirements in responding to Requests Nos. 12(a) and 12(b).

    .. *Charter schools must provide at least as much instruction time during a school year as
       required of other public schools. Accordingly, the minimum number of days of instruction is*

effectively 180. The minimum number of hours in a day that a school must be in session for that day to count as a day of instruction (and against the 180 day minimum) is as follows:

.. *2.5 hours per day for half day kindergarten;*

.. *5 hours per day for full day kindergarten and grades 1-6 exclusive of lunch time; and*

.. *5.5 hours per day for grades 7-12 exclusive of lunch time.*

> Submit your responses to Requests Nos. 12(a) and 12(b) as
> Attachments Nos. 12(a) and 12(b).

13.   **Provide a description of the student achievement goals for the proposed school's educational program.**

Please note the following in responding to Request No. 13.

.. *At the application stage, the State University Trustees, consistent with § 2851(2)(b), require an applicant to provide a description of the educational program's student achievement goals. A description of those goals for your educational program can take any number of forms, including but not limited to the following examples:*

–   *the education program will allow students to meet the Regents' performance goals;*

–   *students will make yearly progress toward mastering the curriculum;*

–   *the education program will position students to outperform their counterparts in equivalent district public schools in key measures; and*

–   *the education program will require students to read and write proficiently.*

.. *If you are chartered, you will be required as part of your Accountability Plan to provide not simply a <u>description</u> of the educational program's goals for student achievement (such as those set forth, above), but the <u>precise</u> goals themselves. You will also be required to set forth an anticipated timetable by which students (or a percentage thereof) will meet each goal. Because the precise goals that you would later be required to provide (if chartered) flow from the description of the goals that you provide here, it is important for you to review the Accountability Plan Guidelines. The Accountability Plan Guidelines are in the Appendix to the Application Kit and also are available from the Charter Schools Institute's web site or by request from the Institute.*

.. *You may, but are not required to, lay out precise numerical goals for student achievement in response to Request No. 13—rather than develop those goals (if chartered) as part of the school's Accountability Plan. Remember, however, that if you do, those goals will become part of your charter, and the school will be required to report on the progress it has made in achieving the goals (both on a yearly basis and upon application for renewal). [§§ 2857(2)(b); 2851(4)(a)]*

.. *It is also important to remember that, in response to Requests Nos. 15 and 16, you will be expected to provide the assessments that you would employ to evaluate whether students are meeting the achievement goals that you describe here and that you will later set forth in more precise form (if chartered) in your Accountability Plan. In other words, you must describe achievement goals in response to Request No. 13 that are measurable.*

.. *The requirement that you describe achievement goals that are measurable is critical, given the requirement (if chartered) to report on progress made towards meeting the achievement goals that are in your charter. [§§ 2851(4)(a); 2857(2)(b)]*

Submit your response to Request No. 13 as Attachment 13.

---

14. **Provide the proposed school's learning standards and curriculum, including a description of the skills and knowledge each student will be expected to attain by the end of each grade (or course) in each year of the charter. In addition, indicate that the education program you have described meets or exceeds the student performance standards established by the Board of Regents.**

Please note the following in responding to Request No. 14.

.. *Your response to Request No. 14 is one of the most important and complex components of your application.*

.. *§ 2851(2)(b) mandates that the school's educational program shall meet or exceed the student performance standards set by the Board of Regents. To meet that mandate, Request No. 14 requires you to make two separate but interrelated showings.*

    – *First, you are required to lay out your school's educational program by setting out your school's specific curriculum that will be taught in each subject area at each grade level. In describing your curriculum, you must not only provide the curricular topics but also the specific skills that a student is expected to attain at each point in a student's progress through the school.*

    – *Second, you must demonstrate that your curriculum will be sufficient to enable a student to score a "3" or "4" on the state assessments adopted by the Regents or (if applicable to your school) to pass any Regents high school examinations. In other words, you must show that the school's proposed curriculum would meet the Regents' performance standards. One way to do that is to "crosswalk" your curriculum with the State Learning Standards that correlate to, and are covered by, those assessments.*

.. *The State Learning Standards that correlate to, and are covered by, Regents' assessments are in the following areas: English Language Arts, Mathematics, Social Studies, Science, and Technology Education. An applicant should therefore perform the "crosswalk" with each of the State Learning Standards in those areas to demonstrate that the proposed curriculum encompasses those standards.*

.. *An applicant may, but is not required to, perform the same crosswalk for the other State Learning Standards for which no assessment, and therefore no performance standard, has yet been established. The State Learning Standards that currently have no related assessment are in the areas of: Family and Consumer Sciences (the former Home Economics), the Arts, Career and Occupational Studies, Physical Education, Health, and Languages Other Than English (the former Foreign Languages). If, however, an applicant states an intention, here or elsewhere in the application, to cover some or all of these State Learning Standards, the applicant will then be required to demonstrate that the school's curriculum covers the standards identified by performing the "crosswalk" for those standards.*

.. *In the past, successful applicants have found the use of a table format to be the most effective manner for accomplishing the two separate but interrelated objectives required by Request No. 14. Accordingly, please use the model form, which is to be found in the Appendix to the Application Kit. Sample alignments are also provided to give you a sense of the level of detail required. The format and sample alignments are also available on the Institute's web site (www.newyorkcharters.org). The use of the prescribed form will greatly assist the Institute in reviewing your application. You may also find that it is a useful organizational instrument for your school.*

.. *The New York State Learning Standards, including those that all applicants must show are aligned with your curriculum, may be found at (www.emsc.nysed.gov/ciai/home.html).*

.. *Some applicants in the past have submitted curricular materials in addition to those that are required in responding to Request No. 14. In the event that you wish to submit additional materials (course books, syllabi, etc.) please submit them as part of your response to Request No. 57 (additional materials).*

> Submit your response to Request No. 14 as Exhibit C.

15. (a) Attach a schedule of the state assessments that the charter school will administer.

Please note the following in response to Request No 15(a).

.. *A listing of all New York State assessments may be found on the State Education Department's web site, http://www.emsc.nysed.gov/ciai/assess.html. In providing a response to Item 15(a), you should review this site, and based on that information, provide a chart of the assessments that the school agrees to administer in each year of its charter. You should also indicate that the charter school would administer any other state-required assessments that are phased in subsequent to the application's submission.*

(b) List which, if any, standardized test(s) would be used by the charter school in addition to the required New York State assessments and explain why such standardized test(s) were selected.

Please note the following in responding to Request No. 15(b).

.. *The Charter Schools Institute strongly recommends that applicants administer annually a nationally normed, standardized test to monitor student performance and progress in English language arts and mathematics. Further information may be found in the Accountability Plan Guidelines.*

.. *In thinking about the assessments you plan to use, you should ensure that your chosen assessments will provide the data needed for you to determine whether the charter school has met the student achievement goals that you described in your response to Request No. 13 (description of student achievement goals) or that you are planning to have (if chartered) as part of your Accountability Plan. You should also consider whether your standardized assessment is aligned to your curriculum, so that test results are (i) valid and (ii) can be used to inform instruction.*

16. Provide the other methods of assessment (beside those indicated in response to Requests Nos. 15(a-b)) that would be used by the charter school. As part of your response, please indicate how these assessments would reliably and verifiably measure student performance and achievement goals. For each such assessment method, please indicate if the data obtained will be used to support the school's application for charter renewal.

Please note the following in responding to Request No. 16.

.. *Any assessment used to measure student learning and achievement or attainment of the school's education goals, if intended to provide data that would support charter renewal (or otherwise demonstrate progress in meeting the student achievement goals), must be externally and independently verified. For alternative, non-standardized assessments, you must provide the procedures and processes to obtain such verification. For instance, if you are planning to use student portfolios (to provide data demonstrating student achievement), and to make assessments of those portfolios, you might wish to provide a rubric for assessing the portfolios as well as a plan for retaining independent evaluations of the portfolios.*

.. *In addition, if you have not indicated that the school would administer annually a nationally normed, standardized test, you should indicate, as part of your response, how the school will be able to demonstrate a student's gain in academic performance on a year-to-year basis.*

.. *As with Request No. 15(b), in thinking about the assessments you plan to use, you should make sure that your chosen assessments will provide the data needed for you to determine whether the charter school has met the student achievement goals that you outlined in your response to Request No. 13 (description of student achievement goals) or that the school would have (if chartered) in its Accountability Plan.*

Submit your response to Request No. 16 as Attachment 16.

17.   **If the charter school would serve the 12th grade within the requested term of the charter, attach a description of the requirements for a student to be awarded a diploma.**

Submit your response to Request No. 17 as Attachment 17.

IV. STUDENT POPULATIONS

18.(a) **Provide the proposed school's methods and strategies for serving students with disabilities in compliance with all federal laws and regulations relating thereto.**

Please note the following in responding to Request 18(a).

.. *As indicated by the request above, § 2851(2)(s) requires that an applicant for a charter school supply the "methods and strategies for servicing students with disabilities in compliance with all federal laws and regulations relating thereto." As a charter school is, for purposes of the Individuals with Disabilities Education Act (IDEA), a school within a local educational agency (LEA), i.e., a school within a school district (or more than one school district if enrolled students with disabilities reside in more than a single school district), the charter school's range of methods and strategies, if they are to be in compliance with federal law, are actually quite limited. A charter school's main obligation is not to create a set of methods and strategies but to work with the school districts to ensure that required services are provided.*

– *In particular, IDEA and the implementing federal regulations, 34 CFR § 300, coupled with § 2853(4)(a) and § 2856(1) of the Education Law, make clear that it is the responsibility of the committee on special education (CSE) of each student's district of residence to conduct initial evaluations of students to determine if they are eligible to receive special education and related services. It is also a CSE's responsibility to design, review and revise the individualized education plans (IEP(s)) mandated by IDEA (with input from relevant school personnel) and to have in place the due process procedures available to students and parents in connection with the above.*

.. *At least two areas of discretion are, however, left to charter schools:*

– *First, a charter school can choose to provide the special education and related services mandated by each enrolled child's IEP, or it can arrange to have such services provided by the student's school district of residence or by contract with a qualified third party provider. Accordingly, you should indicate which entity the charter school contemplates would provide the required services. It is likely, of course, that you envision that the charter school will provide some services while calling upon the district to provide the remainder. You should indicate as best you are able (at this preliminary stage) which services you anticipate the school will provide.*

For instance, you might indicate that the school will retain on a full-time basis one special education coordinator and one special education teacher, and that it is expected that these individuals will provide consultant teacher services and will staff a resource room. You would then indicate that the balance of other services that are mandated by all enrolled students' IEPs would be provided by the students' school districts of residence.

- *Second, a charter school, if it wishes, can, upon notice and consent of a student's parents, seek to have a child's IEP revised by the CSE of the student's district of residence or have the child's status as a special education student re-evaluated. Many charter schools undertake a systematic effort to revise IEPs, believing that in many instances the IEPs in place at the time that children are first enrolled in the charter school are overly restrictive and do not maximize the child's ability to receive a free and appropriate public education in the least restrictive environment. In your answer, you should indicate if the school intends to undertake such a program and describe in general terms the contours of such program. Please remember, of course, that such re-evaluations are conducted by the relevant CSEs and not by the school.*

.. *The federal regulations implementing the IDEA, 34 CFR § 300, are available on line at* http://www.ideapractices.org/idearegsmain.htm

(b) **Please provide the following assurances regarding the provision of special education and other services to children enrolled in the proposed charter school.**

.. **The school will adhere to all provisions of federal law relating to students with disabilities, including the IDEA, section 504 of the Rehabilitation Act of 1974, and Title II of the Americans with Disabilities Act of 1990, that are applicable to it.**

.. **The school will, consistent with applicable law, work with LEA school districts to ensure that all students with disabilities that qualify under the IDEA:**

- **have available a free appropriate public education (FAPE);**

- **are appropriately evaluated;**

- **are provided with an IEP;**

- **receive an appropriate education in the least restrictive environment;**

- **are involved in the development of and decisions regarding the IEP, along with their parents; and**

- **have access to appropriate procedures and mechanisms, along with their parents, to resolve any disputes or disagreements related to the school's or school district's provision of FAPE.**

.. The school will employ, at a minimum, a properly certified individual as the school's special education coordinator, whose responsibilities will include coordinating with CSEs, providing information to CSEs to determine if entering students have IEP, and working with CSEs and school districts to ensure that all required special education and related services are being provided and that all IEPs are appropriate in the context of the charter school setting. The school may permit the special education coordinator to take on additional administrative duties to the extent that they do not interfere with the coordinator's responsibilities to ensure the school's compliance with the IDEA, section 504 of the Rehabilitation Act of 1974 and Title II of the Americans with Disabilities Act of 1990.

.. The school will make available, as required by law, a student's regular and special education teachers (and other required school personnel) for meetings convened by such student's CSE.

.. The school will ensure that parents of children with special needs are informed of how their children are progressing on annual IEP goals and in the general curriculum at least as frequently as parents of regular education children.

.. The school will abide by the applicable provisions of IDEA and the Family Educational Rights Privacy Act of 1974 in order to ensure that data regarding students with disabilities is retained and kept confidential, including having procedures for maintaining files in a secure and locked location with limited access.

.. The school's special education coordinator will retain such data and prepare such reports as are needed by each disabled child's school district of residence or the State Education Department in order to permit such entities to comply with federal law and regulations.

.. The school will comply with its obligations under the Child Find requirements of IDEA, including 34 CFR § 300.125, and will provide appropriate notification to parents in connection therewith, including notifying them prior to providing a child's name to a CSE for potential evaluation.

.. The charter school will not convene its own CSE, make evaluations of children suspected of being disabled, create IEPs, reevaluate or revise existing IEPs or conduct due process hearings. The charter school understands that these responsibilities are left solely to the CSE of the student's district of residence.

.. Appropriate charter school personnel will attend such training and technical assistance seminars regarding the education and servicing of special education students as is required by the State University of New York, including those sponsored by the State Education Department.

Please note the following in responding to Request 18(b).

.. An applicant must provide the assurances set forth above in writing. A statement that it agrees to the assurances is not sufficient.

> Submit your response to Request Nos. 18(a) and 18(b)
> as Attachments 18(a) and 18(b).

19.   Attach a description of the program design, methods and strategies for serving students who are limited English proficient (LEP) in accordance with federal law, including Title VI of the Civil Rights Act of 1964 and the Equal Educational Opportunities Act of 1974. Such description must include the following elements:

..   the process for the identification and placement of students whose first language is not English and the methods for determining the kinds of assistance that these students may need;

..   the manner in which the applicant will ensure that LEP students are not misplaced or tracked inappropriately in other classes (including those programs or classes designed to serve students with disabilities);

..   the description of exit criteria and related objective assessment instruments and subjective methods that will ensure the appropriate student placement and monitoring of a student's progress over time;

..   a description of the educational soundness of the program model pursuant to which LEP students will be provided services, including the authorities upon which the applicant relies to demonstrate that the program is likely to meet the educational needs of all LEP students;

..   a statement that affirms that all students, regardless of language proficiency, will be provided the necessary curriculum and instruction to allow them to achieve to the high standards set for all students in the school;

..   a description of the planned implementation of the program model, including information regarding the allocation of resources to the service of all LEP students including

   –   a description of how staff, curricular materials, and facilities will be used,

   –   a statement that affirms that LEP students will not be excluded categorically from curricular and extra-curricular activities because of an inability to speak and understand English, and

   –   a description of the planned evaluation of the program model over time, including the identification of benchmarks of success (and the corresponding bases for their establishment); the uses of standardized and other assessments; and the related disaggregation of data that will facilitate a program review and the measurement of progress of LEP students over time;

– a description of the planned outreach to parents in the community, including strategies for communicating with parents who are not proficient in English.

Please note the following in responding to Request No. 19.

.. *For the legal requirements regarding the provision of instruction to LEP students, you may wish to review the following publications of the United States Department of Education's Office for Civil Rights: "Policy Update on Schools' Obligations Toward National Origin Minority Students With Limited-English Proficiency (LEP students)," dated September 27, 1991; "Office for Civil Rights Policy Regarding the Treatment of National Origin Minority Students Who Are Limited English Proficient," dated April 6, 1990 (and attaching "The Office for Civil Rights' Title VI Language Minority Compliance Procedures," issued originally December 3, 1985); and "Identification of Discrimination and Denial of Services On the Basis of National Origin," dated May 25, 1970. Each of these publications is available at http://www.ed.gov/offices/OCR/docs/laumemos.html*

.. *For assistance in designing your program of instruction for LEP students, the New York State Bilingual Education Network provides an index of resources at http://www.nysben.org/index.html. In addition, the State Education Department has recently published "The Teaching of Language Arts to Limited English Proficient/English Language Learners: A Resource Guide for All Teachers." This guide is useful; however, it should be used with caution as it references the Commissioner's regulations, with which a charter school need not comply. Copies of this guide can be obtained from the State Education Department's Office of Bilingual Education, Albany, New York, 12234.*

.. *While the above resources are helpful, it is the Institute's experience that an applicant will not be able to provide a satisfactory response to this Request unless they obtain the assistance of someone with experience in designing and implementing programs for LEP students. The Institute strongly urges you to seek professional assistance from qualified personnel. Please note that the Institute's State Stimulus Fund Seed Grant Program is specifically designed to assist applicants in underwriting the costs associated with developing an LEP program.*

> *Submit your response to Request No. 19 as Attachment 19.*

20.   If the proposed charter school includes particular methods, strategies or programs for meeting the needs of students at-risk of academic failure, attach a description of the challenges faced in educating the targeted population and describe such methods, strategies and/or programs. Please include in the description any diagnostic methods or instruments that will be used to identify and assess those students who are performing below grade-level as well as the processes/programs/tools to be used in providing them with remedial instruction.

Please note the following in responding to Request No. 20.

.. *It is probable you have touched upon the methods you will use to identify and educate students at risk of academic failure—in the Executive Summary and elsewhere. Request No. 20 is designed to permit you to expand and provide detail on these topics. The Institute's experience is that a charter school should expect to attract a significant and even, perhaps, a disproportionately large number of children at risk of academic failure who already are several years behind academically. In your response to this Request, you should explain in detail the processes/programs/tools that you intend to use to provide remedial instruction to those children in order to permit them to meet the performance standards of the proposed school and the Regents.*

> Submit your response to Request No. 20 as Attachment 20.

21.   **If the proposed charter school would include any methods and strategies for dealing with other targeted student populations, attach a description of the targeted student population(s), how they would be identified (academic or other criteria) and describe such methods and strategies.**

> Submit your response to Request No. 21 as Attachment 21.

V. PARENTAL AND COMMUNITY INVOLVEMENT

22. (a) **Please describe how parents will be involved in the charter school, including, in particular, the governance and administration of the charter school.**

Please note the following in responding to Request No. 22(a).

.. *§2851(2)(c) states that a charter school applicant must provide the processes "to be followed by the school to promote parental . . . involvement in school governance." Accordingly, while an applicant is required by law to set out those processes, the law does not require any specific governance structure.*

> Submit your responses to Request No. 22(a) as Attachment 22(a)

(b) **Please describe how staff will be involved in the charter school, including, in particular, the governance and administration of the charter school.**

Please note the following in responding to Request No. 22(b).

.. *Education Law §2851(2)(c) states that a charter school applicant must provide the processes "to be followed by the school to promote . . . staff involvement in school governance." Accordingly, while an applicant is required by law to set out those processes, the law does not require any specific governance structure.*

Submit your responses to Request No. 22(b) as Attachment 22(b).

23.   **Provide evidence of adequate community support for and interest in the proposed charter school sufficient to allow the school to reach its anticipated enrollment. Include any methods or strategies that have been used to gauge community support for the charter school.**

Please note the following in responding to Request No. 23.

..   *§ 2851(2)(q) requires an applicant to provide evidence of adequate community support for and interest in the charter school sufficient to allow the school to reach its anticipated enrollment.*

..   *Many applicants find that the most direct evidence of support for their proposed charter school is to gather signatures on petitions. While petitions are a useful method for gauging support, please remember that the evidence you gather should be targeted to showing that your proposal has support sufficient to meet its enrollment goals. In other words, your petition is most effective if it demonstrates that parents of school-age children are interested in potentially sending their children to the school you propose. Consistent with that, your petitions should clearly indicate the purpose of the petition and whether the signatory has school-age children and would be inclined to send children to such a school if it opened. Please note: names of signatories and street addresses will be redacted in the interest of personal privacy and are not subject to disclosure under the Freedom of Information Law.*

..   *While a petition provides perhaps the most direct and compelling evidence that there exists sufficient community support and interest to permit a proposed school to meet its enrollment targets, it is not the only valid evidence. For instance, an applicant might submit a mix of the following: a valid petition; evidence of a desire for alternatives in the school's location; evidence that the alternatives now available are insufficient; and support from community leaders who are willing to provide public support for the school.*

Submit your response to Request No. 23 as Attachment 23.

24.   **Attach an assessment of the programmatic and fiscal impact of the establishment of the proposed charter school on existing public and nonpublic schools in the same geographic area.**

Please note the following in responding to Request No. 24.

..   *§ 2851(2)(q) requires an applicant to provide "an assessment of the projected programmatic and fiscal impact of the school on other public and nonpublic schools in the area."*

..   *At a minimum, the discussion of fiscal impact on public schools should include the dollar amount the proposed charter school anticipates following children from each district*

(AOE/TAPU multiplied by number of students, special education, Title I), the percentage of dollars that represents for each district, and a narrative on programmatic impact. Charter schools may also evaluate the savings that they anticipate a board of education will realize from the reduction in students for which they are providing instruction. Please note that Item 24 also requires you to discuss the fiscal and programmatic impact of the proposed school on nearby nonpublic schools as well.

> Submit your response to Request No. 24 as Attachment 24.

VI. SCHOOL GOVERNANCE

25.   **Attach the charter school's qualifications for service on the school's board of trustees.**

Please note the following in responding to Request No. 25.

..   *§ 2851(2)(c) provides that an applicant must describe the qualifications that the school has for determining an individual's eligibility to serve on the proposed school's board. Oftentimes, it happens that the qualifications of the initial members of the proposed board do not necessarily match the qualifications that the applicant has provided in response to that item. Because the needs of the school may change over time, and therefore the qualifications of the board may also change, the Charter Schools Institute does not view this as necessarily indicating a deficiency (though an alignment is still desirable). If there is a mismatch between the school's qualifications for board membership and the initial board members, the applicant should indicate this fact and explain why this is so.*

> Submit your response to Request No. 25 as Attachment 25.

26.   **List the proposed members of the board of trustees for the charter school, indicating any ex-officio members and any vacant positions expected to be filled. Each proposed trustee who is named must complete the "Request for Information from Prospective Charter School Board Members" contained in the Appendix to the Application Kit.**

Please note the following in responding to Request No. 26.

..   *§ 2851(2)(m) requires an applicant to provide background information on all proposed members of the board of trustees.*

..   *The Appendix to the Application Kit contains the "Request for Information from Prospective Board Members." Each proposed member of a charter school's board of trustees must fill out completely a copy of the Request for Information. The Request for Information is also available on the Institute's website (www.newyorkcharters.org).*

.. *Oftentimes, applicants will reserve certain positions on the school's board for which no individuals can as yet be identified. For instance, it is common for applicants to include, on the School Board, an elected representative of the parents. Where you intend to do so, you should so indicate.*

> Submit your response to Request No. 26 (including completed Request for Information forms) as Attachment 26.

27.   **Please provide a set of by-laws for the proposed school, which includes the charter school's method for appointment/election of trustees and the length of the terms established for each trustee position.**

Please note the following in responding to Request No. 27.

.. *In drafting the proposed charter school's by-laws, please review carefully sections 216-a, 226 and 2853 of the Education Law, noting in particular the intersection between Education Law and the Not-for-Profit Corporations Law. In addition, please remember that charter schools, pursuant to § 2854(1)(e), are subject to the Open Meetings Law, Article 7 of the Public Officers Law. Accordingly, while many not-for-profit corporations' by-laws contain provision that permit trustees to be present through telephonic means or to vote by proxy, the school's legal requirement to follow the Open Meetings Law does not permit such practices. (The Open Meetings Law does permit meetings to be held, with certain restrictions and requirements, by teleconference.) Accordingly, in adapting by-laws from a not-for-profit corporation (or using a model by-laws), be sure that each provision is consistent with the laws applicable to charter schools and their unique status.*

.. *Your by-laws should indicate the committees that the corporation would create, e.g., audit, finance, compensation, etc., and delineate the functions and powers of those committees.*

> Submit your response to Request No. 27 as Exhibit D.

28.   **Attach a description of the responsibilities and obligations of the charter school trustees.**

Please note the following in responding to Request No. 28.

.. *§ 2853(1)(f) provides that the board of trustees of the charter school shall have final authority for policy and operational decisions of the school, but that nothing therein shall prohibit the board of trustees of a charter school from delegating decision making authority to officers and employees of the school in accordance with the provisions of the charter. You may wish, therefore, to discuss in particular those decisions over which the Board of Trustees, as a general matter, intends to retain authority and those it intends to delegate. You may also wish to discuss in more general terms the proposed board's governance philosophy. For instance, you may wish to discuss what is the proper role of the board of trustees.*

.. *Your discussion should also indicate the minimum number of meetings the proposed school's board will meet in each year of the charter. It is the experience of the Institute that fewer than 10 meetings a year does not provide sufficient oversight.*

.. *In discussing the board of trustees' role, you must indicate how the board of trustees is to be kept informed of how the school is doing, including what sources of data it will use to assess that the school is meeting its educational goals and whether the school is operating pursuant to the directives of the board. For instance, will trustees visit the school to make inspections or will they rely solely on the school director's report to the board? If the latter, you should consider and discuss how the trustees will be able to assess and verify the information being provided to you by the school director.*

Submit your response to Request No. 28 as Attachment 28.

29.   **Provide an organizational chart for the school and a narrative description of the chart. The materials supplied should indicate clearly the reporting structure of staff to the board of trustees and staff to the school director(s). If the charter school would contract with a company for management services, explain the company's role in the organizational structure of the school.**

Please note the following in responding to Request No. 29.

.. *Teachers, administrators and other school personnel are required to be employees of the education corporation formed to operate the charter school. Such personnel may not be employees of a management company or other organization that has contracted with the charter school. [§ 2854(3)(a-1)]*

.. *For management company associated schools, applicants are required to provide a specific statement indicating to whom the director of the school reports.*

Submit your response to Request No. 29 as Attachment 29.

30.   **Attach the code of ethics of the charter school. The code of ethics must include a comprehensive and formal conflict of interest policy with specific procedures for implementing the policy and assuring compliance therewith. The code of ethics and conflict of interest policy must be written to apply to trustees, officers and employees of the school.**

Please note the following in responding to Request No. 30.

.. *§ 2851(2)(v) requires that an applicant provide a "code of ethics for the charter school, setting forth for the guidance of its trustees, officers and employees the standards of conduct expected of them."*

.. *Your conflict-of-interest policy may be set forth in the proposed school's by-laws. If so, please so indicate by citing to the appropriate section(s).*

Submit your response to Request No. 30 as Attachment 30.

VII. SCHOOL POLICIES

31. Attach the proposed student admission policy and procedures for the charter school. This
     policy should include, at a minimum, the following information:

     .. the required anti-discrimination criteria and allowable admissions preferences;

     .. the scheduled application and enrollment periods for the first and subsequent years,
         including the approximate date in each year on which you intend to hold the lottery, if
         necessary;

     .. an outreach plan including strategies for publicizing the school and recruiting
         prospective students;

     .. the specific targeted student population (if any);

     .. the step-by-step procedures to be implemented in the event timely applications for
         admission exceed the available spaces, including who will conduct the lottery, the
         precise manner in which the lottery will be conducted, and measures that will be taken
         to ensure that the admission process adheres to § 2854(2); and

     .. the procedures for student withdrawal from the school.

     Please note the following in responding to Request No. 31.

     .. *In scheduling an approximate lottery date in the second or subsequent years, the Institute
         strongly recommends that it occur prior to March 1. This will permit parents time to file
         transportation requests from the school district prior to the April 1 date that school districts
         are permitted by law to impose. [§ 3635] In addition, the March 1 datewill allow both the
         charter school and the school district of location to better plan and budget for the upcoming
         school year.*

Submit your response to Request No. 31 as Attachment 31.

32. Attach the charter school's student discipline rules and procedures for regular education
     students. If your school is to have a provision for suspension or expulsion, include as well
     the procedures and policies for implementing alternative instruction.

     Please note the following in responding to Request No. 32.

.. *Your discipline policy must specify the following: (i) the substantive acts for which a child may be disciplined; (ii) the consequences (or range of consequences) resulting from committing each such act (including suspension or expulsion); (iii) the due process procedures that the school will follow in applying its discipline policy; and (iv) the individuals responsible for carrying out the discipline policy. In addition, you should indicate how the school staff will be educated about, and trained to implement, the policy.*

.. *It is the experience of many charter schools that the creation and effective implementation of the school's discipline policy is highly important to the success of the school. While the amount of material requested in applying for a charter school can often result in the temptation to utilize a model policy not specific to the school, when it comes to discipline, this temptation should, if possible, be avoided. The freedom to shape the school's discipline policy to match the educational vision of the school's leadership team (so long as such policy provides for fundamental due process), is one of the signal advantages given to charter schools.*

.. *Rather than providing a discipline policy that contains only negative consequences for violations of the policy, some schools have integrated into their discipline policy a system of rewards for good conduct. You may want to consider doing this, so that your discipline policy can shape school culture in the broadest possible manner.*

.. *A charter school, like its district public school counterparts, is obligated to provide alternative instruction to students who are suspended or expelled. Under the decisions of the Commissioner, a school should provide alternative instruction to students as soon as practicable. In general, a school is required to provide such instruction by no later than the day after the suspension or expulsion is effective. Such instruction can be at a location and time of the school's choosing, so long as each is reasonable. For instance, a school can choose to provide tutoring to a suspended student at the school or at the student's home, either during the school day or before or after school hours. A school may also provide such instruction at another location, again so long as it is reasonably accessible to the student.*

| Submit your response to Request No. 32 as Attachment 32. |

33.   Please provide the discipline policy that the school will enact for students with disabilities.

Please note the following in responding to Request No. 33.

.. *Charter schools are subject to federal laws and regulations governing the discipline of students with disabilities, including in particular the requirements of the Individuals with Disabilities Education Act and the Department of Education's implementing regulations. These regulations are highly specific as to discipline and the additional due process protections afforded affected students and parents. Accordingly, please review sections 519-529 of Part 300 of Title 34 of the Code of Federal Regulations (34 CFR § 300.519-29). These provisions are available on line at http://www.ideapractices.org/idearegsmain.htm. In crafting your discipline policy, remember that the committee on special education (CSE) is formed by the student's district of residence and that the school must work through and with that CSE.*

.. *Remember also that 34 CFR § 300.527 provides due process protections for a student who has yet to be evaluated by a CSE, but who the school knows may be eligible for referral to a CSE or who is undergoing evaluation at the time of the incident requiring discipline under the charter schoolis policy.*

> Submit your response to Request No. 33 as Attachment 33.

34.   **If the charter school would implement a dress code policy, provide such policy including a description of how the cost of any uniform would be covered for parents unable to afford them.**

> Submit your response to Request No. 34 as Attachment 34.

35.   **Provide a description of the food services to be provided by the charter school.**

Please note the following in responding to Request No. 35.

.. *§ 2851(2)(r) requires that an applicant provide the information requested.*

> Submit your response to Request No. 35 as Attachment 35.

36.   **Describe plans for health services to be provided by the charter school, or options under consideration.**

Please note the following in responding to Request No. 36.

.. *§ 2851(2)(r) requires you to provide the information requested.*

.. *As part of your response, you should specifically indicate the plans and procedures that your school will have for students who require medication at the school every day. Please be advised that boards of education must provide resident children who attend charter schools "any and all of the health and welfare services and facilities which are made available...to or for children attending the public schools of the district."[§2853(4)(a) and § 912] Accordingly, in responding, you may first wish to ask the school district in which you propose to locate for a description of the services that equivalent public schools are currently being provided.*

> Submit your response to Request No. 36 as Attachment 36.

37.   **Attach the proposed school's policies and procedures for complying with the New York State Freedom of Information Law (Article 6 of the New York Public Officers Law).**

Please note the following in responding to Request No. 37.

.. *A charter school must comply with the Freedom of Information Law.* *[§ 2854(1)(e)]*

> Submit your response to Request No. 37 as Exhibit E.

38. **Attach the proposed school's policies and procedures for complying with the New York State Open Meetings Law (Article 7 of the New York Public Officers Law).**

Please note the following in responding to Request No. 38.

.. *A charter school must comply with the Open Meetings Law.* *[§ 2854(1)(e)]*

> Submit your response to Request No. 38 as Exhibit F.

39. **Attach the policies of the charter school's board of trustees for handling complaints from individuals or groups.**

Please note the following in responding to Request 39.

.. *§ 2855(4) provides that any individual or group may bring a complaint to a charter school's board of trustees alleging a violation of any law, including the Charter Schools Act, or of the school's charter. A charter school's board of trustees is therefore obligated to provide the policies and procedures by which these complaints can be handled promptly and fairly.*

.. *A well-fashioned complaint policy will clearly indicate how individuals may present grievances, how those grievances will be reviewed, and who will undertake that task, as well as the timeframe for disposing of a grievance. In addition, the grievance policy must provide adequate notification to individuals of their right to appeal to the Board of Trustees of the State University of New York if they are not satisfied with the handling of their grievance by the school's board of trustees, and, if still unsatisfied, thereafter to the Board of Regents.*

.. *In fashioning your policy, you may wish to review the complaint guidelines of the Board of Trustees of the State University of New York, which are available at the Institute's website, (www.newyorkcharters.org). You may also wish to remember that if chartered, the school would be obligated to follow the policies and procedures that you provide in the application.*

> Submit your response to Request No. 39 as Attachment 39.

40. **In the event of the dissolution of the charter school, attach the procedures that the school would follow for the transfer of students and student records and for the disposition of school assets.**

Please note the following in responding to Request No. 40.

.. *§ 2851(2)(t) of the Education Law requires that a charter school, upon closure or dissolution, must transfer all students and student records to the school district in which the charter school is located—not to each student's district of residence. In addition, it requires that school assets (should any remain) be transferred to either the school district in which the charter school is located or to another charter school within such school district. Transfer of assets to any other entity, governmental, not-for profit corporation or other organization, is not permitted.*

.. *A response that does not set forth specific procedures (approximate timeline, individuals in charge, etc.) but only provides an assurance that the school's procedures will abide by law or repeats the restrictions noted above is not sufficient.*

> Submit your response to Request No. 40 as Attachment 40.

VIII. PERSONNEL

41.   **Attach a copy of the proposed school's personnel policies. The attached policies should include at least the following information:**

.. **the procedures for hiring and dismissing school personnel;**

.. **the school's qualifications for hiring teachers, school administrators and other employees; and**

.. **a description of responsibilities for staff members.**

> Submit your response to Request No. 41 as Exhibit G.

42.   **Provide a roster of instructional staff for the school for each year of the charter that you are seeking. The roster should indicate and identify classroom teachers, and any teaching aides or assistants, as well as any specialty teachers. In addition, the roster should identify the number of instructional personnel in each classroom, e.g., one teacher, one teaching assistant, one paraprofessional for each class. Please indicate as well whether the charter school intends to utilize the limited waiver regarding teacher certification permitted by § 2854(3)(a-1). If so, indicate your understanding of the limitations of that waiver.**

Please note the following in responding to Request No. 42.

.. *§ 2854(3)(a-1) of the Education Law provides that a charter school may hire teachers who are not certified or otherwise approved by the Commissioner of Education, so long as such teachers do not exceed in total more than 30% of the teaching staff or five teachers, whichever is less, and, in addition, each such uncertified teacher fits within one of the* *criteria set forth at § 2854(3)(a-1)(i-iv). While a charter school need not employ any but certified teachers, you may wish to preserve the flexibility granted to you by the law.*

.. *§ 2851(2)(i) requires that a charter school employ at least three teachers after the first year of operation unless the charter school presents a compelling reason why it should not, such as service in a geographically remote region of the State. If you are planning to employ fewer than three teachers in the second or subsequent years of operation, please provide a sufficiently compelling justification.*

> Submit your response to Request No. 42 as Attachment 42.

43.   **If the charter school would have more than 250 students in the first year of operation, indicate whether you are requesting a waiver from the requirement that instructional employees must be members of the existing collective bargaining organization in the school district where the charter school would be located.**

Please note the following in responding to Request No. 43.

.. *§ 2854(3)(b-1) provides that if a school's enrollment in the first year exceeds 250 students, the instructional staff of the school will automatically be certified in a separate bargaining unit of the same employee organization that represents similar employees of the school district in which the charter school is located. The State University Trustees can waive this mandate in up to ten schools that it has authorized.*

.. *If you are requesting the waiver, please note that the waiver will not be given to the school until the school's enrollment actually exceeds the 250 cap in the first year of operation. However, if you do request the waiver and your application is approved with that request, you will have the assurance that the waiver will be granted if needed.*

> Submit your response to Request No. 43 as Attachment 43.

IX. FINANCES AND ACCOUNTABILITY

44.   **Detail a start-up budget for the charter school, including the planned timetable, assumptions for revenue and expenditures, and documentation of start-up revenue. For any funds in the school budget that are provided by an outside source, please provide a letter of commitment detailing the amount and uses for the funding.**

Please note the following in responding to Request No. 44.

.. *To assist the applicants in preparing the start-up budget, the Institute has created a sample start-up budget. The Sample Start-Up Budget is contained in the Appendix to the Application Kit. In addition, the Institute will provide an electronic version of the document upon request. While you are not required to use the Sample Start-Up Budget, you should review it to understand the level of detail that the Institute is seeking.*

.. *In addition to the budget, be sure to include the anticipated timetable and all assumptions used in the calculations. A budget without a full set of stated assumptions cannot be meaningfully reviewed.*

| Submit your response to Request No. 44 as Attachment 44. |

45. **Detail the charter school's proposed first-year annual budget and provide a discussion of the assumptions used to determine revenue and expenditures. Provide as well a cash flow projection on a monthly basis with related assumptions.**

Please note the following in responding to Request No. 45.

.. *To assist the applicants in preparing the first-year budget, the Institute has created a sample first year budget. The Sample First-Year Budget is contained in the Appendix to the Application Kit.*

.. *In addition, the Institute will provide an electronic version of the document upon request. While you are not required to use the Sample First-Year Budget, you should review it to understand the level of detail that the Institute is seeking.*

.. *In addition to your first-year budget, be sure to include a discussion of the assumptions used in the calculations. A budget without a full set of stated assumptions cannot be meaningfully reviewed.*

.. *The cash flow projection should reflect a well thought out timetable of anticipated revenue receipts and expenditure outlays on a month-by-month basis for the first fiscal year. Note that while the fiscal year for a charter school runs July 1 – June 30, in its first year of operation it includes the months prior to July 1 and should be accounted for as such in your projections. In laying out the first-year budget please assume that you would be chartered on March 1st of the year that you are scheduled to commence instruction.*

| Submit your response to Request No. 45 as Attachment 45. |

46. **Provide a five-year budget plan for the charter school, including the assumptions for changes to expenditure and revenue amounts during this period.**

Please note the following in responding to Request No. 46.

.. *To assist the applicants in preparing the five-year budget, the Institute has created a sample five-year budget. The Sample Five-Year Budget is contained in the Appendix to the Application Kit. In addition, the Institute will provide an electronic version of the document upon request. While you are not required to use the Sample Five-Year Budget, you should review it to understand the level of detail that the Institute is seeking.*

.. *Whatever format you choose to use for the five-year budget, the information from Items 44 and 45, above, should be duplicated in the appropriate columns for start-up and first year totals. The discussion of the assumptions should be limited to years 2–5 as the assumptions for the start-up and first-year are already clearly addressed in Items 44 and 45.*

> Submit your response to Request No. 46 as Attachment 46.

47. **Provide supporting evidence that the start-up budget plan, the first-year budget, and the five-year budget plan are sound and that the proposed school would have sufficient start-up funds available to it.**

Please note the following in responding to Request No. 47.

.. *The Charter Schools Act requires an applicant to provide supporting evidence that the fiscal plan for the school is sound. [§ 2851(2)(e)] Some applicants choose to have their financial plan reviewed by an independent certified public accountant, certified financial advisor or other qualified professional. While this is a good way to fulfill the requirement in the Charter Schools Act, it is expensive. In the alternative, applicants can indicate in their response the steps that they have taken to ensure that the fiscal plan is sound. For instance, you could point out that you have been conservative in all assumptions (both in the realization of revenue and potential expenses), that your budget contains a substantial contingency fund, that all revenues are non-contingent or if contingent, discounted, etc. In addition, you can discuss the other ways in which the budget takes into account contingencies in staffing, cost overruns, etc.*

.. *Whether you review the financial plans or that review is conducted by a qualified professional, please note that it is particularly important that you ensure that the personnel, equipment and construction costs that are identified in other parts of your application are included in your budget. For instance, if you have identified a remedial program that includes after-school tutoring, you must provide an entry for costs associated with that tutoring.*

> Submit your response to Request No. 47 as Attachment 47.

48. **Detail the charter school's requirements for the performance of programmatic and fiscal audits.**

Please note the following in responding to Request No. 48.

.. *Audits must, at a minimum, meet the scope of audits required of other public schools, and all audits must be performed at least annually. Note that for the first annual audit, the audit period would include the start-up period through the end of the first fiscal year end, June 30, with the start-up portion of the financials to be identified in the footnotes to the financial statements.*

> Submit your response to Request No. 48 as Attachment 48.

49.   Describe the insurance coverage to be carried by the charter school, including the name of the insured and amounts of insurance for liability, property loss, and student personal injury.

Please note the following in responding to Request No. 49.

..   *§ 2851(2)(o) requires that an applicant provide the types and amount of insurance to be obtained by the school, which shall include adequate insurance for liability, property loss and personal injury of students.*

> Submit your response to Request No. 49 as Attachment 49.

X. SCHOOL FACILITIES

50.   Indicate where the charter school would be located, including complete street address (if known), municipality and school district. If the school would be located within the City of New York, provide the community school district of location.

Please note the following in responding to Request No. 50.

..   *You must have identified, at a minimum, the school district in which a charter school is to be located at the time you file your application. If your charter school is to be located in New York City, you must at a minimum identify the borough of location. A failure to identify the school district (or borough if located in New York City) will result in your application being returned to you as incomplete.*

> Submit your response to Request No. 50 as Attachment 50.

51.(a) If you have already identified a charter school facility, describe the facility, including whether it is new construction, part of an existing public or private school building, or a conversion in use.

> Submit your response to Request No. 51(a) as Attachment 51(a).

(b) If you have not identified a charter school facility, describe plans for doing so. The applicant must notify the Charter Schools Institute within ten days of securing a facility.

> Submit your response to Request No. 51(b) as Attachment 51(b).

52.   If the charter school or its applicants or partners would own or lease its facility, provide a
       description of the ownership or lease arrangement of the facility, including indicating
       specifically any potential conflicts-of-interest and arrangements by which such conflicts
       will be managed or avoided.

> Submit your response to Request No. 52 as Attachment 52.

53.   Provide a description of the charter school facility, or proposed facility, and its layout.
       Include the number and size of the classrooms, common areas, recreational space, any
       community facilities, and any residential facilities (e.g., dormitories or faculty housing).

Please note the following in responding to Request No. 53.

.. *A charter school facility, for purposes of local zoning, land use regulation and building code
compliance, is to be treated as a nonpublic school. [§ 2853(3)(a)] Accordingly, a charter
school need not comply with the requirements of the State Education Department regarding
public school facilities. It need only meet the building code of the locality in which it is to be
sited. Nonetheless, you may find it helpful to access the State Education Department's
facility resource website (*http://www.emsc.nysed.gov/facplan/publicat/bldgaid.pdf*) The
website provides much useful information including recommended square footage for
classroom sizes. In addition the National Clearinghouse for Educational Facilities website
(*http://www.edfacilities.org/*) is also a useful resource tool.*

> Submit your response to Request No. 53 as Attachment 53.

54.   Attach a description of the transportation arrangements made for charter school students,
       including arrangements made for students who would not qualify for public school
       transportation under Education Law, and any supplemental transportation arrangements
       planned with the school district.

> Submit your response to Request No. 54 as Attachment 54.

55.   Describe any intention to expand the charter school, including physical expansion,
       anticipated growth in the school's budget or other financial expansion, expansion in the
       grade levels served, or expected increases in the student population beyond the requested
       time period of the charter.

> Submit your response to Request No. 55 as Attachment 55.

XI. MISCELLANEOUS

56. **Please indicate whether the charter school you propose would:**

    .. **have the same or substantially the same board of trustees and/or officers as an existing private school;**

    .. **draw from an existing private school a substantial portion of the employees of the charter school;**

    .. **would receive from an existing private school a substantial portion of such private school's assets or property; or**

    .. **would be located at the same site as an existing private school.**

    Please note the following responding to Request 56.

    .. *Subdivision 2852(3) forbids the Board of Trustees from approving any application that would involve the conversion of an existing private school to a public charter school, and sets forth the above non-exclusive factors to determine whether a conversion is at issue. If any of the above factors, or any other information, would suggest that your application might involve a conversion, please call the Institute to discuss this issue.*

    > Submit your response to Request No. 56 as Attachment 56.

57. **Please provide, if you wish, any other information that you think would be helpful to the Charter Schools Institute and the Board of Trustees in their evaluation of your application.**

    Please note the following responding to Request No. 57.

    .. *In the event that you feel that the Institute and the Board of Trustees should have other information regarding the charter school that you have proposed, and that such information does not fit within any of the other Requests, you may provide such information in response to this Request. Please note that if the information you provide totals 10 pages or less, you should provide the information as an Attachment. If the information or evidence totals more than 10 pages, you must provide it as an Exhibit.*

    > If your response is ten pages or less,
    > submit your response as Attachment 57
    >
    > If your response is over ten pages,
    > submit your response as Exhibit H.

Source Notes

PROLOGUE: FAITH VERSUS REASON IN EDUCATIONAL REFORM

1. Amy Stuart Wells, *Time to Choose: America at the Crossroads of School Choice Policy* (New York: Hill and Wang, 1993); Peter W. Cookson Jr., *School Choice: The Struggle for the Soul of American Education* (New Haven: Yale University Press, 1994); J. R. Henig, *Rethinking School Choice: The Limits of the Market Metaphor* (Princeton: Princeton University Press, 1994); Joe Nathan, "Heat and Light in the Charter School Movement," *Phi Delta Kappan*, March 1998, v.79, n.7, p.499 (7); Michael Engel, *The Struggle for Control of Public Education: Market Ideology vs. Democratic Values* (Philadelphia: Temple University Press, 2000).

2. Milton Friedman, *Capitalism and Freedom* (Chicago: University of Chicago Press, 1962); Robert B. Everhart, *The Public School Monopoly: A Critical Analysis of Education and State in American Society* (San Francisco: Pacific Research Institute for Public Policy, 1982); John E. Chubb and Terry M. Moe, *Politics, Markets, and America's Schools* (Washington, D.C.: Brookings Institution Press, 1990); Peter W. Cookson Jr., "The Ideology of Consumership and the Coming Deregulation of the Public School System," in Peter W. Cookson Jr. (ed.), *The Choice Controversy* (Newbury, Calif.: Corwin Press, Inc., 1992), pp. 83-99; Chester E. Finn Jr. and Theodor Rebarber (eds.), *Education Reform in the 90s* (New York: MacMillan Publishing Company, 1992); B. Fuller and R. F. Elmore, "Empirical Research on Educational Choice: What Are the Implications for Policy Makers?" in B. Fuller, R. F. Elmore, and G. Orfield (eds.), *Who chooses? Who loses? Culture, Institutions and the Unequal Effects of School Choice* (New York: Teachers College Press, 1996), pp. 187-201; Joseph Lieberman, "Schools Where Kids Succeed," *Reader's Digest*, January 1999; Bruce Fuller

(ed.), *Inside Charter Schools: The Paradox of Radical Decentralization* (Cambridge, Mass.: Harvard University Press, 2000).

3. U.S. Department of Education, www.uscharterschools.org.

4. Willis D. Hawley, "The False Premises and False Promises of the Movement to Privatize Public Education," *Teachers College Record,* summer 1995, v.95, n.4, pp.735–742; Alex Molnar, *Giving Kids the Business: The Commercialization of America's Schools* (Boulder, Westview Press, 1996); Christy Lancaster Dykgraaf and Shirley Kane Lewis, "For-profit Charter Schools: What the Public Needs to Know," *Educational Leadership,* October 1998, v.56, n.2, p.51 (3); Gerald Bracey, *Charter Schools* (Milwaukee: Center for Research, Analysis and Innovation, University of Wisconsin-Milwaukee, 2000); Brett Lane, *Choice Matters: Policy Alternatives and Implications for Charter Schools* (Portland, Ore.: Northwest Regional Education Laboratory, 2001).

5. Peter W. Cookson Jr., *School Choice: The Struggle for the Soul of American Education* (New Haven: Yale University Press, 1994).

6. Chester E. Finn Jr., Louise Bierlein and Bruno V. Manno, "Finding the Right Fit: America's Charter Schools Get Started," *Brookings Review,* summer 1996, v.14, n.3, pp.18–21; Chester E. Finn Jr., Louise Bierlein, and Bruno V. Manno, *Charter Schools in Action: A First Look* (Indianapolis, Ind.: Hudson Institute, 1996); Angela H. Dale and Dave DeSchryver (eds.), *The Charter School Workbook: Your Roadmap to the Charter School Movement* (Washington, D.C.: The Center for Education Reform, 1997); Theodor Rebarber, *Charter School Innovations: Keys to Effective Charter Reform,* Policy Study No. 228 (Los Angeles, Reason Pubic Policy Institute, July 1997); Bryan Hassel, Gina Burkhardt, and Art Hood, *The Charter School Review Process: A Guide for Chartering Entities* (Washington, D.C.: U.S. Department of Education/Southeastern Regional Vision for Education, 1998) ; Bruno V. Manno, Chester E. Finn Jr., Louise Bierlein, and Gregg Vanourek, "Charter Schools: Accomplishments and Dilemmas," *Teachers College Record,* spring 1998, Issue 99, no.3, pp.537–557; Angela H. Dale (ed.) *National Charter School Directory. 1998–1999* (Washington, D.C.: Center for Educational Reform, 1999); Bruno V. Manno, Chester E. Finn Jr., and Gregg Vanourek, "Charter School Accountability: Problems and Prospects," *Educational Policy,* September 2000, v.14, n.4 (21).

7. Definition taken from Employer-Linked Charter Schools Web site: http://www.employercharterschools.com/faqs.htm.

8. *Case Study: Academy for Plastics Manufacturing Technology,* published on the Employer-Linked Charter Schools Web site: www.employercharterschools.org/learn/pubs/plastics.pdf

9. Choice 2000 Charter School Web site: http://www.choice2000.org/

10. Excel Education Centers Web site: http://www.excel.apscc.k12.az.us.

11. *Charter School Highlights and Statistics* (Washington, D.C.: Center for Educational Reform, 2001).

12. Joe Nathan, "Heat and Light in the Charter School Movement," *Phi Delta Kappan*, March 1998, v.79, n.7, p.499 (7).

13. Craig Sautter, *Charter Schools: A New Breed of Public Schools* (Naperville, Ill.: North Central Regional Education Laboratory, 1993); Alan Bonsteel and Carlos A. Bonila, *A Choice for Our Children: Curing the Crisis in America's Schools* (Oakland, Calif.: Institute for Contemporary Studies, 1997); Paul E. Peterson and Bryan C. Hassel (eds.), *Learning from School Choice* (Washington, D.C.: Brookings Institution Press, 1998); Bruno V. Manno, Chester E. Finn Jr., and Gregg Vanourek, "Beyond the Schoolhouse Door: How Charter Schools are Transforming U.S. Public Education," *Phi Delta Kappan*, June 2000, v.81, n.10, pp. 736 (9).

14. *Charter Schools: Changing the Face of American Education* (Washington, D.C.: Center for Educational Reform, 2001).

15. Brett Lane, *Choice Matters: Policy Alternatives and Implications for Charter Schools* (Portland, Ore.: Northwest Regional Education Laboratory, 2001).

16. Herbert Gintis, "The Political Economy of School Choice," *Teachers College Record*, spring 1995, v.96, n.3, pp. 492–511; Seymour B. Sarason, *Charter Schools: Another Flawed Educational Reform?* (New York: Teachers College Press, 1998); Edward B. Fiske and Helen F. Ladd, *When Schools Compete: A Cautionary Tale* (Washington, D.C.: Brookings Institution Press, 2000); Thomas L. Good and Jennifer S. Braden, *The Great School Debate: Choice, Vouchers and Charters* (Mahwah, N.J.: L. Erlbaum Associates, 2000).

PART ONE: THE LANDSCAPE OF CHARTER SCHOOLS

1. National Commission on Excellence in Education, *A Nation At Risk: The Imperative for Educational Reform* (Washington, D.C.: U.S. Government Printing Office, 1983).

2. Judith Areen and Christopher Jencks, "Education Vouchers. A Proposal for Diversity and Choice," *Teachers College Record*, February 1971, v.72, n.3, pp. 327–335.

3. Robert C. Bulman and David L. Kirp, "The Shifting Politics of School Choice," in Stephen D. Sugarman and Frank R. Kemerer (eds.), *School Choice and Social Controversy: Politics, Policy and Law* (Washington, D.C.: Brookings Institution Press, 1999).

4. Ibid.

5. Mary Haywood Metz, *Different by Design: The Context and Character of Three Magnet Schools* (New York: Routledge & Kegan Paul, 1986); Christine H. Rossell, *The Carrot or the Stick for School Desegregation Policy: Magnet Schools or Forced Busing* (Philadelphia: Temple University Press, 1990).

6. People for the American Way, *Buying a Movement Right-Wing Foundations and American Politics* (Washington, D.C.: People for the American Way, 1996).

7. Ted Kolderie, *The States Will Have to Withdraw the Exclusive* (St. Paul, Minn.: Center for Policy Studies, 1990); Nancy Paula, *Improving Schools and Empowering Parents: Choice in American Education* (Washington, D.C.: U.S. Government Printing Office, 1989); David Osborne, "Healthy Competition: The Benefits of Charter Schools," *The New Republic*, October 4, 1999, v.4, n.420, p.31 (3); Simon Hakim, Daniel J. Ryan and, and Judith Stull (eds.), *Restructuring Education: Innovations and Evaluations of Alternative Systems* (Westport, Conn.: Praeger Publisher, 2000).

8. National Commission on Excellence in Education, *A Nation At Risk: The Imperative for Educational Reform* (Washington, D.C.: U.S. Government Printing Office, 1983).

9. Robert C. Bulman and David L. Kirp, "The Shifting Politics of School Choice," in Stephen D. Sugarman and Frank R. Kemerer (eds.), *School Choice and Social Controversy: Politics, Policy and Law* (Washington, D.C., Brookings Institution Press, 1999).

10. Albert Shanker, "Restructuring Our Schools," *Peabody Journal of Education*, spring 1988, v.65, n.3, pp. 97–98.

11. Albert Shanker, *Questions About Charters* (Washington, D.C.: American Federation of Teachers, 1994).

12. Ibid.

13. Susan Urahn, *Minnesota Charter Schools: A Research Report* (St. Paul, Minn.: Minnesota House of Representatives, House Research Department, 1994) (LB2806.U695 1994).

14. Ray Budde, "The Evolution of the Charter Concept," *The Phi Delta Kappan*, September 1996, v.78, n.1, p.72 (2).

15. Peter W. Cookson Jr., *School Choice: The Struggle for the Soul of American Education* (New Haven: Yale University Press, 1994).

16. National Public Radio, transcript from "The Merrow Report," April 4, 1999.

17. Ted Kolderie, *Beyond Choice to New Public Schools: Withdrawing the Exclusive Franchise in Public Education* (Washington, D.C.: Progressive Policy Institute, 1990).

18. *Charter School Highlights and Statistics* (Washington, D.C.: Center for Education Reform, 2001).

19. K. Lloyd Billingsley and Pamela A. Riley, *Expanding the Charter Idea: A Template for Legislative and Policy Reform* (San Francisco: Pacific Research Institute for Public Policy, 1999).

20. John E. Chubb and Terry M. Moe, *Politics, Markets, and America's Schools* (Washington, D.C.: Brookings Institution Press, 1990).

21. Peter Applebome, "New Choices for Parents Start to Change U.S. Education Landscape," *New York Times*, September 4, 1996.

22. Tom Evans, "Education Industry Revenues Top the $100 Billion Mark." eduventures.com, August 2001.

23. Light, 2000.

24. Edward Wyatt, "Investors are Seeing Profits in Nation's Demand for Education," *New York Times*, November 4, 1999.

25. F. Howard Nelson, *How Private Management Companies Seek to Make Money in Public Schools* (Washington, D.C.: American Federation of Teachers, 1997).

26. Robert Lowe and Barbara Miner (eds.), "The Market is Not the Answer: An Interview with Jonathan Kozol," in *Selling Out Our Schools* (Milwaukee : Rethinking Schools, 1996).

27. Andrew Rotherham, "Putting the Needs of our Children First," testimony before the House Committee on Education and the Workforce, Subcommittee on Early Childhood, Youth and Families, May 22, 1999.

28. Abby Goodnough, "Clinton Seeks Some Control of Charter Schools," *New York Times*, May 5, 2000.

29. William J. Clinton, State of the Union address, January 19, 1999.

30. Amy Stuart Wells, Cynthia Grutzik, Sybill Carnochan, Julie Slayton, and Ash Vasudeva, *Underlying Policy Assumptions of Charter School Reform: The Multiple Meanings of a Movement* (New York. Teachers College Record, 1999).

31. Steve Overton, remarks made during panel discussion at 2000 National Charter Schools Conference, Washington, D.C., December 2000.

32. New Dem Daily/New Democrats Online, "Carper Introduces Charter School Bill," March 29, 2001. Washington, D.C.: Democratic Leadership Council.

33. U.S. Department of Education, "Paige Announces $182 Million in Support for Charter Schools," 2001. Washington, D.C.: U.S. Department of Education.

34. *Charter School Laws Across the States* (Washington, D.C.: Center for Education Reform, 2000).

35. *Charter Law Scorecard Ranks States* (Washington, D.C.: Center for Education Reform, 2001).

36. RPP International, *The State of Charter Schools 2000: Fourth-Year Report* (Washington, D.C.: Office of Educational Research and Improvement, U.S. Department of Education, 2000).

37. *Charter Schools: Changing the Face of American Education* (Washington, D.C.: Center for Educational Reform, 2001).

38. Ibid.

39. Joe Nathan, *Charter Schools; Creating Hope and Opportunity for American Education* (San Francisco: Jossey-Bass, 1996).

40. Lynn Schnaiberg, "Charter Schools Struggle with Accountability." *Education Week*, June 10, 1995.

41. Kate Zernike, "Charting the Charter Schools," *New York Times*, March 25, 2001.

42. RPP International, *The State of Charter Schools 2000: Fourth-Year Report* (Washington, D.C.: Office of Educational Research and Improvement, U.S. Department of Education, 2000).

43. James K. Glassman, "Class Acts: How Charter Schools Are Revamping Public Education in Arizona—and Beyond." *Reason,* April 1998, v.29, n.11, p.24 (7).

44. *Charter School Legislation: Profile on Arizona's Charter Law* (Washington, D.C.: Center for Education Reform, 2000).

45. Robert C. Bulman and David L. Kirp, "The Shifting Politics of School Choice," in Stephen D. Sugarman and Frank R. Kemerer (eds.), *School Choice and Social Controversy: Politics, Policy and Law* (Washington, D.C., Brookings Institution Press, 1999).

46. Chester E. Finn Jr., Bruno V. Manno, and Gregg Vanourek, *Charter Schools in Action: Renewing Public Education* (Princeton: Princeton University Press, 2000).

47. Robert C. Bulman and David L. Kirp, "The Shifting Politics of School Choice," in Stephen D. Sugarman and Frank R. Kemerer (eds.), *School Choice and Social Controversy: Politics, Policy and Law* (Washington, D.C., Brookings Institution Press, 1999).

48. Ibid.

49. Bess Keller, "College's Chartering of Schools Upsets Cap in Michigan," *Education Week*, March 14, 2001.

50. Ibid.

51. Chester E. Finn Jr., Bruno V. Manno, and Gregg Vanourek, *Charter Schools in Action: Renewing Public Education* (Princeton: Princeton University Press, 2000).

52. *Charter School Laws Across the States* (Washington, D.C.: Center for Education Reform, 2000).

53. Susan Moore Johnson and Jonathan Landman, "Sometimes Bureaucracy Has Its Charms: The Working Conditions of Teachers in Deregulated Schools," *Teachers College Record*, February 2000, v.102, n.1, pp.85–124.

54. William H. Clune, "Educational Governance and Student Achievement," in William H. Clune and John F. Witte (eds.), *Choice and Control in American Education*, Vol. 2: *The Practices of Choice, Decentralization, and School Restructuring* (New York: Falmer Press, 1990), pp. 391-423.

55. *Charter Schools: Changing the Face of American Education* (Washington, D.C.: Center for Educational Reform, 2001).

56. Chester E. Finn Jr., Bruno V. Manno, and Gregg Vanourek, *Charter Schools in Action: Renewing Public Education* (Princeton: Princeton University Press, 2000).

57. Ibid.

58. *Charter Schools: Changing the Face of American Education* (Washington, D.C.: Center for Educational Reform, 2001).

59. Chester E. Finn Jr., Bruno V. Manno, and Gregg Vanourek, *Charter Schools in Action: Renewing Public Education* (Princeton: Princeton University Press, 2000), p. 76.

60. Ibid.

61. Darcia Harris Bowman, "NSBA Report Casts Critical Eye on Charter Movement," *Education Week*, October 18, 2000.

62. Darcia Harris Bowman, "Michigan Charter Schools Scoring Lower," *Education Week*, November 15, 2000.

63. *Charter Schools: Changing the Face of American Education* (Washington, D.C.: Center for Educational Reform, 2001).

64. RPP International, *The State of Charter Schools 2000: Fourth-Year Report* (Washington, D.C.: Office of Educational Research and Improvement, U.S. Department of Education, 2000).

65. *Charter Schools: Changing the Face of American Education* (Washington, D.C.: Center for Educational Reform, 2001).

66. Paul Hill, et al., *A Study of Charter School Accountability* (Washington, D.C.: U.S. Department of Education Office of Educational Research and Improvement, 2001).

67. Ibid.

68. Amy Stuart Wells, *Beyond the Rhetoric of Charter School Reform: A Study of Ten California School Districts* (Los Angeles: University of California at Los Angeles, 1998).

69. Chester E. Finn Jr., Bruno V. Manno, and Gregg Vanourek, *Charter Schools in Action: Renewing Public Education* (Princeton: Princeton University Press, 2000).

70. Peter W. Cookson Jr., Catherine Embree, and Scott Fahey, *The Edison Partnership Schools: An Assessment of Academic Climate and Classroom Culture* (Washington, D.C.: National Education Association, 2000).

71. Carol Ascher, Robin Jacobowitz, and Yolanda McBride, *Charter School Access: A Preliminary Analysis of Charter School Legislation and Charter School Students* (New York: Institute for Education and Social Policy, New York University, 1999).

72. Carol Ascher and Nathalis Wamba, *Charter Schools: An Emerging Market for a New Model of Social Equity?* Paper delivered to the Conference on School Choice and Racial Diversity, Teachers College, Columbia University, May 22, 2000.

73. Chester E. Finn Jr., Bruno V. Manno, and Gregg Vanourek, *Charter Schools in Action: Renewing Public Education* (Princeton: Princeton University Press, 2000).

74. Eric Rofes, *How Are School Districts Responding to Charter Laws and Charter Schools?: A Study of Eight States and the District of Columbia* (Berkeley: Policy Analysis for California Education, 1998).

75. James K. Glassman, "Class Acts: How Charter Schools are Revamping Public Education in Arizona—and Beyond," *Reason*, April 1998, v.29, n.11, p.24 (7).

76. RPP International, *Challenge and Opportunity: The Impact of Charter Schools on School Districts* (Washington, D.C.: Office of Educational Research and Improvement, U.S. Department of Education, 2001).

77. Richard Rothstein, Peggy Farber, and Ross Corson, "Charter Conundrum," *The American Prospect*, July-August 1998, n.39, p.46 (15).

PART TWO: THE SOCIAL AND POLITICAL GEOLOGY OF CHARTER SCHOOLS

1. Robert B. Everhart, *The Public School Monopoly: A Critical Analysis of Education and State in American Society* (San Francisco: Pacific Institute, 1982).

2. C. Wright Mills, *The Power Elite* (New York: Oxford University Press, 1956).

3. Randall Collins, "Functional and Conflict Theories of Educational Stratification," *American Sociological Review*, 1971, Issue 36: pp. 1002–1019.

4. John Meyer, "The Effects of the Institutionalization of College in Society," in K. A. Feldman (ed.), *Selected Readings in the Social Psychology of Higher Education* (New York: Pergamon, 1972), pp. 109-261.

5. Jean Elshtain, *Democracy on Trial* (New York: Basic Books, 1995).

6. Ibid., p. 14.

7. Nancy Paulu, *Improving Schools and Empowering Parents: Choice in American Education* (Washington, D.C.: U.S. Government Printing Office, 1989).

8. Robert Putnam, *Bowling Alone: The Collapse and Revival of American Community* (New York: Simon and Schuster, 2000).

POSTSCRIPT: THE GOODNESS OF AMERICA— AN EDUCATION FOR DEMOCRACY

1. Peter W. Cookson Jr. "Fostering Moral Democracy," *Educational Leadership*, October 2001. vol. 59, n.2, pp. 42-45.

2. Peter W. Cookson Jr. "First Person Plural: Education as Public Property," *Social Class, Poverty and Education*, Bruce J. Biddle (editor). New York: Routledge Falmer, 2001, pp. 31-48.

Index